Stars Over
MONTANA

Stars Over
MONTANA

A Centennial Celebration of the
Men Who Shaped Glacier National Park

WARREN L. HANNA
Published in cooperation with the Glacier Association

TWODOT®

GUILFORD, CONNECTICUT
HELENA, MONTANA
AN IMPRINT OF THE GLOBE PEQUOT PRESS

A · T W O D O T® · B O O K

Text design: Sheryl P. Kober
Layout: Joanna Beyer
Project manager: John Burbidge

Library of Congress Cataloging-in-Publication Data
Hanna, Warren L. (Warren Leonard), 1898-1987.
Stars over Montana : a centennial celebration of the men who shaped
Glacier National Park / Warren L. Hanna.
    p. cm.
"A TwoDot Book."
Originally published: West Glacier, Mont. : Glacier Natural History
Association, c1988.
Includes bibliographical references and index.
ISBN 978-0-7627-4903-4
1. Glacier National Park (Mont.)—Biography. 2. Glacier National Park
(Mont.)—History. I. Title.
F737.G5H37 2009
978.6'52—dc22

                                                          2008045824

Printed in the United States of America

10 9 8 7 6 5 4 3 2 1

In loving memory of my late husband,
Warren L. Hanna, who prepared this book as a tribute
to all devotees of Glacier National Park, and in honor
of the surviving family members of the men who
were the author's inspiration.

Frances R. Hanna

Contents

Foreword

Even today, it's easy to imagine the sense of awe that was awakened in the early pioneers seeing the land that is now Glacier National Park for the first time. The men featured in this book looked up toward those dizzying heights, explored the lakes and valleys, and marveled at the open ice fields, and then they took steps to preserve and protect the land for future visitors.

As the Glacier Association, we are dedicated to furthering their vision through our mission to "Advance Stewardship of Our Natural and Cultural Heritage through Education and Interpretation." We are delighted to make the stories of these "Stars Over Montana" available as a tribute to these men and to the writer of this book, Warren L. Hanna, who was a long-time friend of Glacier National Park, as well as a meticulous historian and engaging storyteller.

—The Glacier Association

Preface

Lovers of Glacier National Park—and they are legion—have come to regard this paradise of mountains, lakes, and trails as a special reserve created by nature for their personal enjoyment. They return to it year after year, or as often as possible, to renew themselves by inhaling its invigorating atmosphere and by climbing, or simply contemplating, its stupendous peaks.

As they become more familiar with the history of the park, they realize they have been preceded by many others in their appreciation of, and love for, this million acres of God's country which crown the United States.

Perhaps the earliest of these aficionados was the legendary Hugh Monroe, whose life in the Northwest spanned more than 75 years of the 19th century, who kept succumbing to the lure of the Glacier Park region throughout his life, and who died not far from the Two Medicine Valley, in which stood his special mountain, Rising Wolf. He loved so well the two bodies of water the Indians called the "Lakes Inside" that he named them St. Mary, after the best-loved of all Catholic saints.

The St. Mary country similarly attracted many of his offspring, some of whom lived in or near the area long before it became a national park. Some of them, including Angus Monroe and Billy Jackson, spent a good part of their lives helping to make it more attractive and enjoyable for those of us who have followed in their footsteps.

Because the park is a region of superlative beauty, it is not surprising that it has appealed to several giants of American art. Charles Russell, the internationally renowned painter and sculptor, discovered its charm before it became a national park. He built within its boundaries his own rustic cabin, where he spent a part of each summer at both work and play. Other major artists, such as Winold Reiss, Hart Merriam Schultz (Lone Wolf), and John Clarke, gained much of their inspiration from time spent in or near the park.

One of the attractions of the park has been its proximity to the Blackfeet Indian Reservation and the talented people who live there. Hugh Monroe, James Willard Schultz, Walter McClintock, Father Pierre Jean DeSmet, and even Charles Russell lived among the Indians—often for years—and so spent much time in or near the future park. Several of those who have been closely associated with the park are themselves part Indian, such as Billy Jackson, Angus Monroe, Hart Merriam Schultz (Lone Wolf), Joseph Kipp, John Clarke, and Thomas Dawson.

Three men have played major roles in the discovery and development of the region. They brought it to public attention and ultimately to national park status, and they created the facilities that allow almost two million visitors to enjoy the area each year. They are James Willard Schultz, George Bird Grinnell, and Louis Warren Hill.

Schultz, known by the Indians as Apikuni, or Appekunny, was the first of this remarkable trio to visit the region and to recognize its tremendous potential. His abilities as writer and guide brought the area to the attention of many. Alone and with others, he explored its peaks, lakes, and valleys, named many of its scenic features, and had several of those features named for him, including the Appekunny Formation, an important type of rock found throughout the park. In later years, Schultz wrote three books dealing directly or indirectly with the park, but perhaps one of the most important things he did was to interest George Bird Grinnell in the region.

Grinnell, a well-known editor, publisher, hunter, explorer, and ethnologist, visited the St. Mary region on a hunting expedition with Schultz in 1885. He became so enthralled by the area's stunning beauty that he continued to visit often and, together with Schultz, he discovered and explored Montana's two largest glaciers, one of which was named for him. It was Grinnell who campaigned long and vigorously to have the area designated as a national park, finally succeeding in 1910. His final visit to the park was in 1926, more than 40 years after his original hunting trip.

The third member of the luminous trio, Louis Warren Hill, was president and later chairman of the board of the Great Northern Railway, which bordered the park on the south. When federal red tape promised to delay the opening of the park for years, Hill intervened. He put the power of his great company behind his determination to establish hotel and highway facilities within the park at the earliest possible moment. Then he put his advertising talent to work publicizing its numerous attractions.

This book contains a series of meticulously researched profiles, mini-biographies of the people who have played important roles in the history of Glacier National Park. Through their lives, one can develop a deeper understanding of the park itself.

—Warren L. Hanna

Acknowledgments

Unfortunately, Warren did not live long enough to see this book in print. However, a number of individuals gave of their time and expertise so that his final publishing project could become a reality. I am deeply indebted to them.

I would especially like to extend my appreciation to the following: the Glacier Association, for accepting the original manuscript; Jack Holterman, author of *Place Names of Glacier/ Waterton National Parks,* for sharing his expertise; and Mel Ruder, a very dear friend who worked closely with Warren on all his Glacier Park publications.

I would also like to thank the following for providing the historical photographs which illustrate *Stars Over Montana:* Gordon Pouliot; Joyce Clarke Turvey; David Andrews, of the James Willard Schultz Society; the Montana Historical Society; and the Minnesota Historical Society.

All of the above have helped to place another Star Over Montana.

May the Warren L. Hanna Star brighten our lives.

—Frances R. Hanna

1
Hugh Monroe
The White Blackfeet

Hugh Monroe was perhaps the first white man to set foot in what is now Glacier National Park. Monroe came to the Northwest from Quebec in 1815 to work for the Hudson's Bay Company. He is credited with naming the St. Mary lakes, which straddle the park's eastern boundary. *Courtesy of Montana Historical Society*

American history is sprinkled with thrilling stories of adventure and romance. Prominent among them is the tale of Rising Wolf, the white Blackfeet Indian who found fame in the shadow of the great peaks of what is today Glacier National Park.

Rising Wolf, or Mah-kwo-i-pwo-ahts, was the Blackfeet name for a lad who came from eastern Canada to work for the Hudson's Bay Company in the wilderness. He found a home with the fiercest tribe that roamed the vast plains just east of the Rockies and became widely known and respected by all the tribes of northwestern Montana during the 19th century. Rising Wolf was the first known white man to set foot upon what is today Glacier National Park, and he became an intermittent resident along its eastern border.

Rising Wolf was baptized Hugh Munro, according to parish records. But when he crossed into the United States he became known most often as Monroe, a spelling his many descendants have accepted and used.

Much of what is known about Monroe has been told by his good friend, James Willard Schultz, who wrote several books about Rising Wolf's adventures in the Northwest. Despite being written about 15 years after Monroe's death and probably from memory, they seem accurate on many points.

According to Schultz, Hugh Monroe was born at Three Rivers, Quebec, on July 9, 1798, to Captain Hugh Monroe of the British Army and Amelie de la Roche, daughter of a noble family of French *émigrés*. Parish records, on the other hand, indicate he was born in L'Assomption, Quebec, on August 25, 1799. His parents are listed as Hugh Munro, a merchant, and Angelique Larocque, a widow before her marriage to Munro. L' Assomption was a suburb of Montreal, where, according to Schultz, Monroe's maternal relatives were bankers and property owners.

Monroe's mother, born Angelique Le Roux, was a member of an old French family that had lived in Canada for more than a century. She was married twice, the first time to Francis Antoine Larocque who, at the time of his death October 31, 1792, was a member of the Quebec legislative assembly. Her second marriage, to Hugh Munro, took place May 4, 1793.

The elder Munro, a merchant at the time of his son's birth, also had a record of military service. In *My Life as an Indian*, Schultz said he was a colonel in the British army. But in three later books, he described him as "Captain Hugh Monroe of the English Army."

Military records indicate Monroe was captain of a company of the Second Battalion of the King's Royal Regiment of New York in 1778. He later moved to Canada and re-entered military service during the War of 1812, serving with the Imperial Forces of the Dominion and retiring as a lieutenant. He died in 1825 of "inflammation of the breast." His prolonged absences from home during the War of 1812 prompted his father-in-law to arrange for Hugh, Jr., and his mother to live with him in Montreal during the war.

As the only child of well-to-do parents, Hugh, Jr., enjoyed his early years in L' Assomption, but he apparently liked Montreal less. In an interview with the *River Press* of Fort Benton, Montana, published February 19, 1890, he said he had attended the English school at Montreal for three years and the priests' college for more than four years, so he probably knew both English and French before leaving the area.

This bilingual ability was to stand him in good stead in later years; however, it was not the type of learning for which he then yearned. Before reaching his teens, he had become a hunter and the proud possessor of a light smoothbore gun that carried 30 balls to the pound. He killed his first deer during his 12th summer and two black bears by the time he was 13. An Indian taught him to trap beaver, otter, and land-roving fur-bearers, such as the fox, marten, and mink. His grandfather Le Roux sold the pelts for him in Montreal. His catch one winter alone netted him 30 pounds, a good sum in those days.

After one of young Monroe's relatives told of his adventures as a fur trader in the "Indian territories," Hugh began to frequent the Hudson's Bay Company warehouses in Montreal, where he was able to mingle with *voyageurs* and trappers from faraway places—men dressed in buckskin clothes with strangely fashioned fur caps on their heads and beaded moccasins on their feet. Some were French and some English, and he spent many pleasant hours listening to their tales of fights with the Indians, encounters with fierce bears, and perilous canoe trips on madly running rivers.

Young Hugh soon resolved that this was the type of life he wanted to lead, and he began to beg his parents for permission to go to work for the great company. At first his pleas fell on deaf ears, but eventually he overcame his parents' objections. He promised his mother he would return after his first tour of duty— a promise he did not keep. His mother prepared a traveling kit that included a prayer book. His father gave him a brace of silver-mounted pistols in holsters for the belt and plenty of ammunition, and his grandfather gave him 20 pounds and a sunglass.

When it was time for his half-brother, Joseph Larocque, to return to the West, Hugh went along to serve a three-year term as an apprentice-clerk for the company in what is now Alberta, Canada. The trip took more than a year. Hugh's party traveled along the Ottawa River, Georgian Bay, Lake Superior, and Rainy River to Fort Garry (now Winnipeg), then by Lake Winnipeg and the Saskatchewan River to Edmonton House, a post which had been established in 1795 on or near the site of present-day Edmonton.

The party consisted of five boats, each loaded with four or five tons of goods for the Indian trade, everything in waterproof packages. The heavy goods were mostly guns, powder and ball, flints, tobacco, beads, traps, axes, rings, kettles, and small hand mirrors. The lighter goods consisted of blankets, brightly colored woolen cloth, needles, awls, thread, and trinkets the traders hoped would appeal to the Indians' fancy.

The party left Montreal in May 1814, and reached York Factory on the Saskatchewan in September, not far from where the river enters Hudson Bay. There they had to winter, resuming their journey in the late spring and eventually reaching their destination in midsummer of 1815. Hugh was not quite 16 years old.

At Edmonton House, young Monroe was taken under the wing of the factor, Richard Hardesty, who had known both his father and grandfather. Eagerly, the boy began to learn the daily routine at the post, even as he marveled at the thousands of Indians who were camping outside the carefully guarded gates, patiently waiting their turns to trade their winter's catch of furs for some of the goods that had arrived from Montreal. He was to learn, among many strange things, that the daily diet at the post consisted of buffalo meat and strong black tea—with plum pudding served at Christmas.

Although the possibility of such an adventure had never crossed young Hugh's mind, he did not hesitate to accept when the company offered to let him spend a year with the Pikuni, or Piegan, tribe of Blackfeet Indians so that he could learn their language and become a proficient interpreter for trading purposes. He would be under the protection of Lone Walker, a Pikuni chief, and would share his lodge, which already housed eight of his 19 wives and their children. Thus, he became part of a great Indian caravan as it headed southward toward the plains of what is now Montana.

Actually, the company assigned young Hugh to live with the Pikunis for three reasons. Not only was he to learn the language so that he might serve as an interpreter in lieu of the totally inadequate Antoine Bissette, a French-Iroquois half-breed whose Cree wife knew a smattering of the Blackfeet language. He was also to see that the tribe returned to Edmonton to trade each year, as well as to check out a rumor that American traders had been pushing westward, seeking to establish posts along the upper Missouri in Blackfeet territory.

In *Rising Wolf: The White Blackfoot*, Schultz said the assignment to live with the Indians was made within a few short weeks of Hugh's arrival at Edmonton House. Some have questioned the time span, but nothing in the Hudson's Bay Company records refutes the assertion. Of course, it is not really necessary to know whether the amazing adventure with his new Blackfeet friends had its beginning two weeks or two years after he reached the Northwest. The point is that his assignment was one with which Hugh was delighted.

The young man's pleasure was enhanced by the friendliness of the Indians. This rapport likely stemmed from three factors: First of all, he was young, attractive, and amiable. Secondly, he was the protégé of Lone Walker, chief of the Small Robes, a major band of the Pikunis, and great chief of all the Blackfeet tribes. Finally, influential tribe members discovered early in the relationship that Hugh possessed personal and unusual influence over the sun, the god of the Blackfeet.

This latter discovery occurred during a noontime stop on the tribe's first day out of Edmonton House. Hugh watched a frustrated medicine man try in vain to light his pipe from a piece of partly charred punkwood. Recalling the sunglass his grandfather had given him, Hugh quickly took it from his pouch and focused it upon the tobacco in the pipe. Soon a thin streak of smoke rose from it. When the medicine man and nearby chiefs saw this miracle, they began crowding around Hugh, seeking to touch this godlike being who obviously possessed special influence with the sun. The news soon spread, and before long Hugh was being called "Natowap-anikapi," meaning "sacred youth." The sunglass had assured his importance with the tribe.

After leaving Edmonton House, young Monroe and the caravan of some 800 lodges traveled by easy stages along the foot of the Rockies to Sun River, where they wintered. The boy had quickly adapted to the daily life of the tribe, and he particularly enjoyed hunting buffalo and other game. He soon developed a special friendship with Chief Lone Walker's son, Red Crow, who was about his age. Together, they experienced many adventures, including an incident in which he saved Red Crow's life by shooting an attacking grizzly—a fortunate feat which served to enhance Hugh's standing with the tribe considerably.

In the spring, instead of returning to the Saskatchewan, the tribe crossed the Missouri River, hunted in the Yellowstone country that summer, wintered on the Missouri at the mouth of the Marias River, and returned to Edmonton House the following spring with all the furs the horses could carry. During this time, Hugh had acquired a good knowledge of the language as well an honorable name, Rising Wolf, given him because of his bravery in a battle with the Crows in the Yellowstone country. He could also report that he had encountered no American traders in Blackfeet territory.

During the two years he was gone, the company had found another interpreter. So Hugh was ordered to remain with the Pikuni tribe to see that it came annually to Edmonton to trade its winter cache of furs. Nothing could have pleased the young man more, and he told his friend, Schultz, many years later that "everyday of that life was a day of great joy."

Young Monroe began to feel even more at home with the tribe, eventually becoming a member of the Aiinakix, or Seizer, band of the All Friends Society. This was an elite group whose members served as tribal policemen, keeping order in the camp and seeing that the people obeyed the hunting rules—a difficult task at times. Occasionally he accompanied Pikuni war parties in forays against other tribes, and once, according to Schultz, he traveled with a party of some 200 warriors to the vicinity of present-day Great Falls, where they unexpectedly encountered noted frontiersman Jim Bridger, together with a dozen trappers and a few Shoshone, or Snake, Indians. With great difficulty, Monroe restrained his Blackfeet companions from attacking and destroying their hated enemies, the Shoshone, as well as the rest of the party.

During these exciting years, Monroe became the first white man to traverse the plains between the Upper Saskatchewan and Upper Missouri Rivers, as well as the first to see many parts of the mountains between the Missouri and the Yellowstone. Since the laconic records of the Hudson's Bay Company continued to list him as an "apprentice" until 1818–19, it seems fair to assume that his job as roving ambassador with Lone Walker and the Pikunis covered the same period. In 1819–20, the records show he made "at least two trips from Edmonton House to Beaver River taking a supply of pemmican," suggesting that his travels with the Pikunis ended then and he was assigned other duties, such as transporting supplies and trade goods between company posts.

During his stay with the Pikunis, probably when he was 19 or 20, Monroe fell in love. As an occupant of Lone Walker's lodge, he had for some time admired the chief's attractive daughter, Ap'-ah-ki, some three years younger than himself. She was slender with a comely face, beautiful eyes, long hair, and graceful movements. The young man fell into the habit of looking at her when he thought no one was watching him, and before long he found he preferred to stay in the lodge, where he could be near her. Nonetheless, they never spoke, since, under the Blackfeet code, it was unseemly for youths and maidens to do so.

Hugh's hopes that they might set up a lodge together were dashed one evening when he heard a suitor offer Lone Walker 30 horses for Ap'-ah-ki's hand. Although the chief turned him down, Hugh thought the refusal of 30 horses removed any possibility for his own hopes, since he did not even own the horse he rode. One day, however, he and Ap'-ah-ki chanced to meet away from the camp and, after a spontaneous embrace, they decided they must go to her father and tell him of their infatuation. The chief smiled and readily gave his consent, telling them he had rejected the previous suitor because he wanted Monroe for his son-in-law. In the words of Schultz, presumably quoting Monroe:

> *That very day they set up a small lodge for us and stored it with robes and parfleches of dried meat and berries, gave us one of their two brass kettles, tanned skins, pack saddles, ropes—and all that a lodge should contain. And, not least, Lone Walker told me to choose 30 horses from his large herd. In the evening we took possession of our home and were happy.*

After the Blackfeet equivalent of a marriage ceremony, the happy couple enjoyed a long and fruitful life together. It ended finally with the death in 1874[1] of Ap'-ah-ki, also known as Sinopah (Kit Fox Woman). The couple are attributed with having 10 children, nine of whom records show survived to maturity despite the hardships of frontier life. As pieced together from various sources, including the complete census of the Pikuni tribe (1907–1908–1909) and other reliable records, the nine survivors were:

- John, the oldest son, born circa 1820. He fathered four children by his first wife, Isabel, including Maggie Collins, Belle Liebert, Magdelaine Favel, and William. Much later, after Isabel's death, he married Christine Delray, a young Canadian woman of French-Cree extraction, whose Indian name was Blanket Woman. To this union, two children were born, Angus in 1887 and another boy who died in infancy.

- Felix, who fathered five children and served in 1859 as principal guide and Blackfeet interpreter for the Palliser expedition of Canada. His nephew, Angus, said Felix also served the Hudson's Bay Company as an interpreter, and he finally froze to death.

- Mary, also known as Margaret, who married Edward Housman and was the mother of three children, James, Hugh, and Maggie.

- Minnie, who became the wife of Alex Fox and is said to have lived to 1923 or later.

- Oliver, sometimes referred to as Olivier, who served with the Palliser expedition in 1859. According to the records of the expedition, members first looked upon him "as a fool," and they were surprised and pleased when he mollified a group of trouble-seeking Blackfeet braves.

- Amelia, frequently called Millie, who married Thomas Jackson, an employee in two or more early trading posts. She bore two children, Robert in 1854 and William in 1856. Both served as scouts for General George Armstrong Custer in the Black Hills in 1874 and in the vicinity of the Little Bighorn in 1876. Later they served in a similar capacity with General Nelson Miles.

- William, also known as Piskan, Peskan, or Piskun, who was the third Monroe brother to serve with the Palliser expedition, having been brought into the group July 4, 1859, by his brother, Felix. He served as the prototype for the hero of one of Moberly's adventures entitled "When Fur Was King."

- Lizzie, the mother of three children, who was married and widowed twice. She lived with her parents after the death of her second husband and is said to have survived to a very old age. She owned a smallbore rifle, was an excellent marksman, and loved to hunt and trap. She once told her father she intended to be a leader in war against Pikuni enemies, as was the Blackfeet warrior maiden, Running Eagle.

- Frank, also known as Francis, Francois, and Heavy Eyes, who was the youngest of Hugh's offspring, born in 1846. He married three times, twice to women of Cree descent and the third time to Mary, a full-blooded Pikuni. He had a son, Frank, by his first wife and five children by his third wife. Frank encountered a grizzly bear in the Two Medicine Valley and barely escaped alive. Although he was crippled in the attack, he is said to have lived to 1923 or beyond.

Schultz credits Hugh with having six children—three sons and three daughters. However, he probably never knew of Felix, Oliver, and William, who spent their adult years in Canada.

Returning to the 1820s, records of the Hudson's Bay Company indicate Hugh Monroe continued to work at Edmonton House in an unspecified capacity. However, he made at least one trip to Rocky Mountain House (then called Acton House) with trade goods between May 17 and July 28 in the company year 1820–21. For the next two years, according to the records, he was employed in the Bow and Saskatchewan districts in unspecified capacities. The termination of his employment in 1823 seems to coincide with charges filed against him involving theft of liquor.

Upon leaving the Hudson's Bay Company, Monroe could either return to tribal life or chart a new course. Fortunately, there was at least one new course to which he could agreeably turn: He could become a hunter and trapper, catering to the world's insatiable appetite for furs and, at the same time, indulging his boyhood passion for the outdoor life of guns and traps.

The company's cryptic records provide some indication he decided on this latter direction. For the period between the company years 1822–23 and 1831–32, Hudson's Bay listed Monroe, when he was shown at all, as a "freeman." In frontier parlance, this meant that he was a "free trader," an independent contractor or freelance hunter and trapper, rather than an employee.

This change in Monroe's lifestyle was momentous; he had to depend entirely upon his own resources, but he was also free to move into new areas and make new contacts. He had come to know the country fairly well, including the better trapping areas. His experience and maturity made it possible for him to operate independently and even form friendships with Indians from tribes outside the Blackfeet Confederacy.

During his early years in the Northwest, probably in the 1820s, Monroe did form such a friendship with members of the Kootenai tribe, which lived west of the Continental Divide. The relationship was to become even more meaningful, in some respects, than the one he had with the Blackfeet.

Little appears to have been written about this unusual friendship with the Kootenais. Why should this white Blackfeet become intimate with an unaffiliated tribe whose home territory west of the Rockies made it a very distant neighbor?

After all, he still was attached to the Blackfeet tribe through his Pikuni wife and children. It seemed a strange and inexplicable relationship.

However, there were a number of explanations for the Monroe-Kootenai friendship. To begin with, the Kootenais were more peaceable and friendly toward white men than most tribes of the Northwest, an important consideration when Monroe was trapping alone with his family at Lower St. Mary Lake. The Kootenais often approached the lake through a mountain corridor from the west, and their friendship gave him a sense of protection from that direction.

Secondly, Monroe occasionally arranged with the hostile Blackfeet to allow the Kootenais to hunt buffalo east of the mountains in plains country regarded by the Blackfeet as their exclusive domain. Finally, the Kootenais and Monroe shared a devout belief in Catholicism, and it was this factor that probably played the leading role in their relationship.

Monroe himself, speaking for publication in the 1890s, said he first met the Kootenais when he discovered and named the St. Mary lakes, an event that, on two occasions, he said took place in 1836. However, the date is doubtful, since Monroe was working for the Hudson's Bay Company in Canada—several hundred miles north of the St. Mary country—for several years before and after 1836. It is also difficult to believe that Monroe could spend 20 years or more in the Northwest prior to 1836 without having visited the St. Mary lakes. And by 1890 Monroe's memory for dates was becoming notoriously erratic. Perhaps he was confusing 1826 with 1836.

The evidence indicates that Monroe met the Kootenais much earlier, perhaps during his first three years with the company. When the factor at Edmonton House sent him to travel with the Blackfeet the second time, he also told him to try to find the Kootenai tribe and induce its trappers to bring their beaver skins to Edmonton instead of to Northwest Fur Company posts along the Columbia River. This may have been in 1817 or 1818.

The 1830s brought competition to the southern Blackfeet territory for the Hudson's Bay Company. Monroe learned in 1832 that the American Fur Company had established a trading post called Fort Piegan at the mouth of the Marias River. Soon after, Monroe went with his family to the fort to lay in a stock of tobacco and supplies, as well as to visit with the post's white traders and perhaps to learn as much as possible about this new and—to the Hudson's Bay Company—revolting development.

Whether the arrival of the American Fur Company on the Marias had anything to do with it or not, Monroe went back to work for the Hudson's Bay Company as an interpreter in 1832, not long after his visit to Fort Piegan. His contract to work in the Saskatchewan District, at 25 pounds a year, was renewed periodically throughout the decade.

The onset of the 1840s found Monroe and his family comfortably established at company headquarters on the north Saskatchewan. But in 1844 he was again a free trader on Lower St. Mary Lake, where the fish and game were plentiful and his Kootenai friends could look in on him readily without fear of encountering hostile forces.

Not long after his return to the lower lake, Monroe had an experience that he regarded as one of the highlights of his life. In August or September 1845, in the presence of some of his Kootenai friends and in the shadow of a huge cross of pine, Monroe christened the sister lakes St. Mary. Since then, a controversy has arisen over how the christening took place and who participated. The story of that controversy appears in the next chapter.

In the 1850s, Monroe and his family continued to lead a gypsy lifestyle, although he did take time out in 1853–54 to serve as guide and interpreter for the exploration party of Governor Isaac Stevens. The party's primary objective in the area was to find a practical railroad route over the Rockies, and members sojourned at Fort Benton for several months while they conducted the search.

After hearing vague stories about a low mountain pass called Marias, Governor Stevens got an accurate description of it and its general location from Little Dog, a Pikuni chief. On the basis of this information, he dispatched reconnaissance parties to seek its exact location. One of them approached from the west in October 1853, while the other was ordered to move southward in May 1854 from above the St. Mary lakes (mistakenly referred to by the party as Chief Mountain lakes), with instructions to skirt the eastern side of the Rockies until the entry to the pass had been reached. Both endeavors failed.

As Monroe had made local history in 1845 with his dramatic christening of the St. Mary lakes, he now had an opportunity to change the course of American history. As guide and interpreter, he was aware of the expedition's search for Marias Pass, and he could have led the way to the pass easily. Instead, although fully aware that Marias Pass had been shunned by nearby tribes for decades (as Little Dog had already explained to Stevens), Monroe warned against the search, saying the party might be ambushed in the pass by hostile Indians. The reasons for this prevarication he carried with him to his grave.

As a result of his advice, the party approaching from the west took a wrong turn and missed the pass. The Marias remained lost to railroad exploration parties for another 36 years. Monroe lost another chance at fame, and the statue that stands now at the summit of Marias Pass is not of Hugh Monroe, but of John Stevens (no relation to Isaac), who discovered it for his employer, the Great Northern Railway Company, in December 1889.

During part of the 1850s and 1860s, Monroe and members of his family worked for the American Fur Company at its Fort Benton trading post. Located there for some years, in addition to Hugh and his wife, Sinopah, were their oldest son, John, with his wife, Isabel; their daughter, Amelia, with her husband, Thomas Jackson, and their children; their youngest daughter, Lizzie; and their unmarried son, Frank. Jackson was the post tailor, and Monroe, assisted by his two sons, was the post hunter.

The 1860s brought a profound change in the affairs of the post. The manager for the American Fur Company, Andrew Dawson, had injured his back in a fall in 1858, and by 1864 he had retired to his native Scotland. With the change in command, Monroe decided to return to trapping beaver in the mountains, and he insisted that his entire family go with him.

Their caravan left the fort one morning in the spring of 1864. In addition to more than 20 packhorses, they had another 70 free horses which Frank and the Jackson boys herded at the rear of the column. Monroe led the procession, and at intervals along the line of horses rode John, Isabel, Amelia, Tom, Lizzie, and Sinopah.

Heading north in the general direction of what is now Glacier National Park, the caravan arrived in a few days in the Two Medicine country. Here, the Jackson boys had their first opportunity to use the new lightweight rifles their father had given them. They had a narrow escape from death when they wounded a huge grizzly which continued, nevertheless, to charge them. Just as it was about to kill the older boy, Monroe came to the rescue and fired the fatal shot.

While still in the Two Medicine Valley, the Monroes were joined by a large party of friendly Kootenais, with whom they visited for a time. Then the families moved on to the foot of Lower St. Mary Lake, where they set up three lodges on the north side of the outlet. Each lodge was made of new, well-tanned, buffalo-cow leather. John and his wife, Isabel, occupied one. Monroe, Sinopah, Frank, and Lizzie had the second, while the Jackson family had the third.

For several weeks they concentrated on trapping beaver. Monroe's sons and grandson, Robert Jackson, worked down the river, while Monroe, Lizzie, and grandson Billy Jackson trapped the little streamlets running down the big ridge into the lake. For awhile, they averaged 10 beaver a day. When the catch had dropped to three or four, they decided to move on to the upper lake. In the meantime, Lizzie had shot a fat young moose, upon which they were feasting the evening disaster struck.

It is ironic that Monroe's favorite campground on the lower lake—the scene of memorable moments in 1845—could also be the setting in 1864 for the most devastating experience of his life. As the family enjoyed the delicious roast in the lodge of Lizzie and her parents, it began to hear the snorting of horses in the corral and the sharp, fierce barks of its dogs. Monroe's two sons snatched up their rifles and hurried into the night to discover that an Assiniboine war party was unfastening the bars to the corral to steal the horses.

After telling the women to run through the timber and down to the ford of the river, Monroe, his two grandsons, and their father, all now fully armed, sallied forth. Lizzie trailed secretly along behind. The Monroes were greatly outnumbered, and the Assiniboines succeeded in making off with all but two of their 100 horses. The raiders then set fire to the lodges and all the Monroes' belongings, except four women's riding saddles which they contemptuously tossed aside. The Assiniboines took with them saddles, traps, beaver skins, cans of powder, sacks of ball, and everything else of value.

Day was breaking by the time the family gathered cautiously at the campsite. A gentle wind brought them the strong odor of burned leather. The growing light revealed desolation. Almost everything they owned had been burned or taken, and three little piles of charred leather and lodgepole ends were all that remained of their lodges. Sinopah sat down and cried inconsolably.

Grief-stricken, Sinopah and Amelia mounted the two remaining horses, and the family started south on the trail that ran over the ridge. Near sundown of the following day, they arrived at lower Two Medicine Lake and found that the Kootenai Indians whom they had left there had broken camp and gone down the river. They took up their trail the next morning, and late in the afternoon they came upon their camp at the mouth of Little Badger Creek.

The surprised Kootenais gave them a sympathetic welcome, as well as a grand feast of boiled buffalo boss ribs, pemmican, stewed *pommes blanches,* and large servings of dried camas roots. They also graciously gave them horses and equipment. Thus refreshed and remounted, the Monroes and Jacksons were able to move south to join the main body of the Pikunis near Bear River. A few days later, they trailed into the Fort Benton river bottom.

So less than 90 days after leaving Fort Benton, the Monroes were back again, bereft of everything with which they had departed, except for the clothes on their backs, their guns, two of their horses and saddles and, of course, the Kootenai gifts. New plans had to be made, and Tom Jackson, who did not relish the life of a trapper, decided to resume his job as post tailor. Monroe and his sons elected to get new traps, ammunition, and other necessities on credit at the post and to head immediately for the Belt Mountains. The Jackson boys accompanied them.

The men trapped along the upper reaches of Deep Creek and along the Judith and Musselshell Rivers, finally returning to Fort Benton in November laden with six packs of beaver skins. Each pack weighed 90 pounds. This was a pattern of life from which they were not to deviate for several years. They trapped from early spring to late fall and then spent the winter comfortably in their old quarters at the post. Monroe would never work for anyone but himself again.

The dawn of the 1870s found Monroe and his family in their winter quarters at Fort Benton, comfortable but somewhat disenchanted. The little settlement was continuing to grow, and soldiers now occupied the old adobe fort. A store or two, several saloons, a hotel, and a number of cabins and log houses had sprung up. The discovery of gold elsewhere in the territory was attracting a horde of newcomers.

Early in 1870, Monroe began once more to feel the urge to wander. In April, he headed north again with his family, which now included the Cree wife of Frank, a newlywed. The Jacksons, despite much urging, declined to go along. Tom Jackson decided that he and his family would move down the Missouri to Fort Buford, where he thought he could find employment.

The Monroes traveled to the headwaters of the South Saskatchewan River, better known as the St. Mary lakes. In the region nearby, buffalo still roamed in seemingly endless numbers. The neighboring valleys teemed with elk, deer, and smaller game. High in the adjacent uplands, flocks of wild sheep and goats were plentiful. Best of all, as Monroe well knew, these were the haunts of the mighty moose, which supplied him with his favorite meat. For Monroe, this "wilderness were paradise."

During the 1870s, trappers were getting generous cash payments for the pelts of timber wolves. In their first season at the St. Mary lakes, the Monroes collected more than 300 of them to pack to Fort Benton, where they brought five dollars each. They also caught many beaver, otter, mink, marten, and fisher.

Monroe's method of trapping the wolves was simple and unique. He built oblong, pyramidal log pens about 8 by 16 feet at the base and 8 feet in height. He placed the top layer of logs about 18 inches apart. Easily climbing the slope of these traps, the wolves would jump down through the narrow apertures at the top to feed upon the meat placed inside as a decoy. Then they would be unable to escape. Often, Monroe and his sons would find several big wolves in the trap each morning. They would kill and skin them and peg the hides out to dry on the ground.

The St. Mary locale had one disadvantage: Small, roving bands of Crows, Yanktonnais, or Assiniboines might attack anytime. This made it necessary for the Monroes to keep their horses in a strong corral just behind their lodges at night, and to post a watch during the day as their horses grazed on the rich prairie grasses. Each of the Monroes, including the women, had guns, flintlocks, and a good supply of powder and ball. Although they were always able to fend off these sporadic attacks without any casualties, the Monroes sometimes did not venture far from camp.

For the most part, however, these were pleasant days. The living was easy and the scenery sensational. The trip to St. Mary country in 1870 began the longest and perhaps most profitable of Monroe's stays at his favorite retreat. Unfortunately, like all good things, the happy years there could not go on forever.

The year 1880 found Monroe and his family still leading an independent, nomadic existence. However, the routine of the year was broken in its latter months, when for the first time Monroe met James Willard Schultz. Young Schultz had just returned from a visit to his former home in New York to find the Pikunis encamped along the Missouri River at the mouth of what they called Creek-in-the-Middle. As Schultz told the story:

I had heard much of a certain white man named Hugh
Monroe or, in Blackfeet, Rising Wolf-Mah-kwo-i-pwo-

ahts. One afternoon I was told that he had arrived with his numerous family, and a little later met him at a feast given by Big Lake. In the evening I invited him over to my lodge and had a long talk with him while we ate bread and meat and beans, and smoked numerous pipefuls of tobacco. We eventually became firm friends.

According to Schultz, Monroe told him that he had never revisited his home in eastern Canada and that he had never seen his parents after the day they had parted from him at the Montreal docks. He had intended to return for a brief visit at some time, but he kept deferring it. Then he had received letters, two years old, saying both his parents were dead. He also got a letter from an attorney, saying they had bequeathed him a considerable amount of property, and that he should go to Montreal to sign the necessary papers that would entitle him to its possession.

At about that time, the company factor at Mountain Fort was going to England on leave. A trusting Monroe gave him power of attorney. The factor never returned, and Monroe lost his inheritance. He did not mind much, for he had a lodge and family, good horses, and a vast domain teeming with game within which to wander—a domain extending from the Saskatchewan to the Yellowstone and from the Rockies to Lake Winnipeg.

The 1880s saw the disappearance of the buffalo and, thus, privation and hardship for all the Montana tribes. For aged Hugh Monroe, these were the years of his decline, as well. He became destitute and dependent upon friends and relatives for support. Always resourceful, he decided in the summer of 1888 to go to Fort Macleod, Alberta, to ask the Hudson's Bay Company for financial assistance. He was astute enough to enlist the services of Johnson and Johnson, attorneys of that community who drafted a formal petition for him. It read as follows:

To the Honourable
the Governor of the Hudson Bay Company

The Petition of the Undersigned Humbly Sheweth:

That your Petitioner entered into the service of your Honourable Company in 1796 and remained in said service for the long period of seventy years having been employed as clerk interpreter and trader among the Cree and Blackfeet Indians in the vicinity chiefly of Fort Edmonton in the Northwest Territories of Canada.

That when he retired from the service of the Company his salary was over two thousand dollars in arrears.

That he has repeatedly applied for payment to the Edmonton agent but was put off from time to time and has not received his said salary or any part of the same.

That he is now far advanced in life and unable to earn his own living and is dependent on the charity of the public for the necessities of life.

That he is of great age of One hundred and eight years. Your Petitioner therefore prays that it may seem good to your Honourable Company to grant him a small quarterly allowance of money sufficient, at least, to maintain him and give him a decent burial and your old and faithful servant will ever pray.

Signed in the presence
of Wm Johnson, Advocate
and Notary Public at
Fort McLeod this 27th day of June A.D. 1888
Wm Johnson
Notary Public
[signed] Hugh Munro

To reinforce his appeal, Monroe sought the assistance of the celebrated Father Albert Lacombe, and the latter's letter dated June 21, 1888, to Joseph Wrigley, the Hudson's Bay Company trade commissioner at Winnipeg, is of great interest. It read as follows:

I will take the liberty to write to you, in favor of an old servant of the Hudson Bay Co. His name is Hugh Mounroe; born at L' Assomption, near Montreal. He is almost one hundred years old. When he was a young man he came in this country and was for many years, at the service of the Company, in the great and important district of Edmonton, of fort Auguste or fort des Prairies. It was in the time of the famous chief factor, John Rowan.

Mounroe was a favorite of the Blackfeet and of the other Indian tribes of the plains. He get married with a maiden of the piegan band. Then he left Edmonton to live among the Indians, always at the employment of the H. B. Co., as interpreter and trader. He got a large family, sons and daughters, whom some are yet alive.

Now the old man is round this place, infirm and miserable having nothing to live on, except what he receives from the white people and from some friendly Indians. That's really a pity and a shame to see that poor old man, who one day was so much in favor with your company, having some education, smart and gentle, knowing English, French, Blackfeet, Cree languages, now destitute and abandoned. Of course that's his own fault. The money he made, was wasted by carelessness and foolishness. As he has only short time to live, I thought to call to your charity and generosity in behalf of Hugh Mounroe. If you think advisable for

the H. B. Co. to grant him some thing, it might be better
to give him so much a month from the store.

The petition and the letter went through company channels, and on August 9, 1888, Commissioner Wrigley wrote
Father Lacombe, saying he would not recommend a pension,
but he had instructed the officer in charge of the company post
at Fort Macleod to see that Monroe "does not suffer from star-
vation or want. Mr. Gigot will occasionally make him presents
of food and clothing."

It is doubtful that Monroe ever benefited from this com-
mitment. Company records contain no further reference to his
case, although Monroe lived more than four years longer, to
December 8, 1892. Available information indicates he spent all
those years in the United States, and it is extremely unlikely
he ever again made the long trek to Fort Macleod to take advantage of the occasional handouts the company had promised.

Correspondence in this case gives a conflicting picture of
Monroe in 1888. Father Lacombe characterized him as "smart
and gentle," although "infirm and miserable." Attorneys Johnson and Johnson described him as "quite active" and his mental faculties as being "in considerable vigour." Chief Factor
Richard Hardesty wrote: "For the last 20 years he has been in
his dotage, and consequently but little reliance can be placed
on what he says." The most interesting description of Monroe
is to be found in this excerpt from a letter dated July 12, 1888,
from E. F. Gigot, officer in charge of the company post at Fort
Macleod:

He wanders about from place to place, very feeble and
infirm in body, but he still has lots of mental energy in
him and is wonderfully intelligent and clearminded for
a man his age. He is a favorite with Indians and white

*men and lives on charity all the year around, although
I have never known him to ask for anything . . . There
is no doubt that he is a very pitiful object and awak-
ens sympathy. He must have been a magnificent man
physically in his day, and even yet is a noble wreck.*

This episode in Monroe's life is notable for what it discloses
about him in his later years. In the petition signed by him before
a notary in 1888, he alleged not only that he was 108 years old,
but also that he had been in the company's employ for 70 years
commencing in 1796. Apparently he did not consider that the
company records, if they were checked, would show he had
entered its service in 1815 as an apprentice at age 16, verifying
that he had not even been born in 1796. Moreover, while these
same records would show a substantial period of employment
by the company, the total was 20, rather than 70, years. He did
not work for the company at all after 1844.

Files of Montana newspapers show that in the year 1890 he
was publicly claiming to have been born in 1784 and, thus, was
a centenarian. Apparently, he had found it convenient to forget
that he had told his friend Schultz he was born in 1798. He also
seemed to prefer forgetting that his father had married his only
recently widowed mother in 1793, as records would attest.

Monroe had presumably discovered that claiming to be
Montana's oldest man was enough to make him an object of
great public interest, and hopefully, for the purposes of his
petition, an object of special sympathy. Fortunately for Monroe, the company did not check its records as to his claims;
however, the amount of sympathy which he succeeded in gen-
erating did not result in a single dollar of the pension which he
had hoped to obtain.

The beginning of the 1890s found Hugh Monroe back
within a few miles of the southeastern comer of what is now

Glacier National Park. A newspaper story appearing in February 1890, a few months after his 90th birthday, reported that he was living on the Two Medicine River near the Pikuni Indian Agency with two of his sons. According to his grandson Angus, Hugh's oldest son, John, had moved his family to the area in 1887 or 1888 because he had been able to get work with the Holy Family Mission, probably as a caretaker or groundskeeper. Residents of the area received their mail at the mission, and James Willard Schultz, who lived with his wife, Natahki, on a small ranch about four miles down the river, took advantage of frequent mail trips to visit extensively with old Hugh Monroe at John's nearby home.

During these years, usually in September or October, John Monroe and his friends—including the Schultzes—would head for the Two Medicine Lake area to lay in a winter's supply of the game which was so plentiful in the vicinity, including elk, deer, and bighorn sheep. Until his last year, Rising Wolf accompanied them on horseback, although he had to be helped into the saddle. According to Angus, his grandfather mostly smoked a pipe in camp and kept tabs on the meat gathering. At night, he slept in his son's tent.

The Fort Benton *River Press,* in a February 1890 article about Monroe, described him as vigorous and able to mount a horse with the agility of a boy. He occasionally went to the mountains with his son to fetch firewood and on his own to a nearby stream to catch trout. He still had his old flintlock gun, a smoothbore of great length that he fondly called "Queen Anne." He also carried an old Scotch dirk. The article humorously concluded that "he never belonged to a Montana legislature which, with his other temperate and virtuous traits, may account for his longevity."

At the time of this 1890 interview, although he had only just passed 90, he claimed to be 106 years old. When interviewed in October 1892 by the Chinook *Opinion*, he claimed to be 108. He was living at the time across from the railroad station at Midvale (now East Glacier), where he occupied a tent next to a log cabin in which one of his sons lived. The *Opinion* article said, "There is nothing peculiar about living in a tent, except that this man has lived in one much of the time for ninety years."

Observations by the Montana press and others during the early 1890s paint an excellent picture of Monroe in his twilight years. He was described as about five feet six inches in height, blue-eyed, originally fair-haired, with a square chin and a rather prominent nose. His long life on the plains had given him a few scars from old arrow wounds, and he had lost sight in his left eye as the result of an encounter with a Sioux Indian.

Following his death December 8, 1892, from unreported causes, the Choteau *Montanian* printed the following obituary:

Word has just been received stating the death of Hugh Monroe, who has long been known as the oldest man in Montana.

Mr. Monroe, who lived on Two Medicine Creek, four miles north of the agency, on Blackfeet Reservation, in Chouteau County, was born near Montreal, Canada, May 4, 1784, and was therefore over 108 years of age at the time of his death, which occurred on Thursday last, 8th inst. At the age of 18, he started west with a relative, in the employ of the Hudson Bay Company, and was stationed on the Saskatchewan River. In 1806 Monroe married a Blackfeet woman and left the employ of the company to dwell among the Indians.

Much of his early life was spent among the Kootenais. In 1832, having heard of the arrival of the

American Fur Company's traders at the mouth of the Marias he made a long journey with his wife, to again see white man and lay in a stock of tobacco. In 1836 with a party of Kootenais, he discovered St. Mary's lake, erecting a large cross there at the time.

In 1853 Gov. Stevens' survey party landed at Fort Benton, and Monroe acted as guide and interpreter as far as Walla Walla (Washington), from which point he returned to the Kootenais.

About 10 years ago Monroe returned to the Blackfeet reservation, and later took up his residence on Two Medicine Creek, about 50 miles east of the main range of the Rockies.

Very few interpreters could equal him as a sign talker, and he spoke various Indian languages fluently. Up until a few days before his death he was quite active for a man of his age, and was an inveterate hunter. He rarely visited the white people, and for 90 years past his life was spent almost entirely with the Indians.

In the light of current information, the obituary contains several errors. The claim that he was born in 1784 was preposterous, as was his claim to be 108. He actually lived to be 93, a ripe enough old age, and obviously even his long life among the Indians did not add up to 90 years.

Moreover, Monroe was 15 when he started west, not 18. And he did not leave "the employ of the company" in 1806 and marry a Blackfeet woman. He did not even arrive in the Northwest until 1815, and he took a wife four years later. While he probably discovered the St. Mary lakes much earlier than 1836, his christening of them in the presence of Kootenai friends did not take place until 1845.

Even Monroe's death has become the subject of confusion. His biographer, James Willard Schultz, in his introduction to *Rising Wolf: The White Blackfoot*, had the following to say: "He died in his ninety-eighth year, and we buried him in the Two Medicine Valley."

Only two pages earlier, Schultz wrote that Monroe had been born July 9, 1798, which would mean he had died in 1896. In a subsequent magazine article, he said, in reference to Monroe's children:

> *They finally all married, and in his old age he lived with one and another of them until his death in 1896, in his ninety-eighth year.*

Since Schultz was among those who helped to bury his old friend in the Two Medicine Valley in December 1892, it is unfortunate that he should have erred repeatedly by a full four years.

It is unfortunate, also, that no gravestone identifies the final resting place of this remarkable pioneer. Angus Monroe said his grandfather's remains lie in an unmarked grave in the burial ground adjacent to the Holy Family Mission in the Two Medicine Valley. Since the cemetery is closed to the public, he could not point out the exact site.

Hugh Monroe was a colorful and fascinating character— one whose life of adventure also became one of controversy. He, more than any other man, bridged the historical gap between the visit of Captain Meriwether Lewis to the upper Marias River in 1806 and the coming of the Iron Horse to Marias Pass in 1891.

He was the first white man not only to visit the park region, but to make a semi-permanent home along its eastern border. The noble peak, Rising Wolf, bears testimony to his early presence in the Two Medicine Valley, and in bestowing the name of St. Mary upon his favorite lakes, he became the first of his race to christen any feature of the future park. When death at last overtook him, it found him but a few miles away from the landmarks he so dearly loved.

2

The Man Who Christened
the St. Mary Lakes

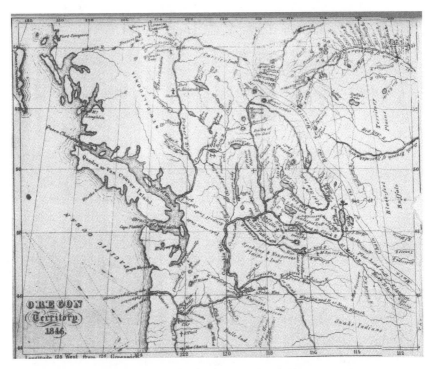

Father Pierre Jean DeSmet has often been mentioned as a participant in the christening of the St. Mary lakes. Yet this map from his book, *Oregon Missions and Travels Over the Rocky Mountains, 1845–1846,* indicates that he never even crossed south of the U.S.–Canadian border in the year the event apparently took place. *Courtesy of Montana Historical Society*

A fascinating riddle in Montana history revolves around the naming of the St. Mary lakes. For more than a century, aficionados of Glacier National Park have puzzled over the who, what, when, and why of this mystery, described in *Through the Years in Glacier National Park*:

> *There is much controversy over the origin of this name as applied to the St. Mary lakes . . . James Willard Schultz states in his writings that Hugh Monroe took Father DeSmet to the lakes and that the priest erected a cross there and gave them their name. However, various historians who have studied Father DeSmet's diaries and journals state that nowhere . . . does he make any mention of the St. Mary lakes, which he most assuredly would have done, had he seen and named them.*

Playing leading roles in the controversy were three of the most colorful characters in early Montana history. The central figure was Hugh Monroe, the celebrated "white Blackfeet" whose extraordinary career in the Northwest spanned more than three-quarters of the 19th century. A shadowy member of the cast was Father Pierre Jean DeSmet, the noted pioneer priest who brought religion to thousands of natives on both sides of the Rockies. The last of the trio, and a major contributor to the controversy, was James Willard Schultz, a fur trader and Monroe's biographer.

The St. Mary lakes provided a brilliant setting for this historical drama. Sitting astride the eastern boundary of the Park, they were the first of its 250 lakes to be discovered and named by a white man. The upper lake, its head nestled against the Continental Divide, is considered by many to be the most exquisite body of water on the North American continent.

Fortunately, many parts of the story of the christening of St. Mary lakes are undisputed. No one denies that a christening ceremony did take place in the wilderness, that it was staged before a cross of logs erected near the lower lake, and that

Monroe participated. The controversy revolves around these questions: Did a Catholic priest take part in the christening? If so, who was he and what part did he play? When did the ceremony take place?

Schultz, in all his reports of the event, claims a priest was involved. However, Monroe never mentions a priest, and books written by or about Father DeSmet fail to mention Monroe, the lakes, or a ceremony.

So, how did such conflicts arise?

Monroe and Schultz Were Good Friends

Schultz and Monroe were good friends, and Schultz had many opportunities to obtain complete and accurate information about every phase of Monroe's life. When Schultz was working for Joe Kipp at Fort Conrad on the Marias River in the early 1880s, Monroe would come to visit for weeks at a time with Kipp's mother, Earth Woman, and her companion, Crow Woman.

Later, Monroe lived alternately with his oldest son, John, near the Holy Family Mission, and with his grandson, Billy Jackson, on the Cut Bank River. Schultz saw much of him at both places, but no one knows what Monroe told Schultz nearly a century ago. Undoubtedly, the old man's adventures at the St. Mary lakes were the subject of more than one conversation between them.

Monroe Tells His Story to Others

Schultz was not the only person Monroe told about the christening of the St. Mary lakes. George Bird Grinnell, editor of the journal *Forest and Stream* and a visitor to the St. Mary area on several occasions between 1885 and 1892, spoke with him about the incident and wrote about it in two magazine articles.

The first, entitled "The Chief Mountain Lakes," appeared in *Science* magazine August 12, 1892. In it, Grinnell stated that "the name (St. Mary lakes) was given them nearly 50 years ago by Hugh Monroe, an old Hudson's Bay Company man." Nothing was said about the participation of a priest, the erection of a cross, or the presence of Kootenai Indians. "Nearly 50 years ago" would place the date at approximately 1845, or at least between 1842 and 1847.

Grinnell also mentioned the incident in an article entitled "The Crown of the Continent," written in 1892 but not published until September 1901 in *Century* magazine. It said: "Here, 48 years ago, Hugh Monroe, a devout Catholic, assisted by a party of Kootenai Indians, set up on the shores of the lower lake a great cross made of two pine trees, and called the lakes St. Mary's."

Again, the report makes no mention of a priest, and again the date is uncertain. If the christening took place 48 years before the article was written, the year would have been 1844.

Montana Newspaper Articles

The first public disclosure of how the St. Mary lakes were named came in the February 19, 1890, issue of the Fort Benton *River Press*. Based on an interview with Monroe, the article said that, "In 1836, being then with his friends, the Kootenai, he discovered and christened St. Mary's lake. He created a large cross there at the time." No mention was made of a priest.

In the October 29, 1892, issue of the Chinook *Opinion*, he was quoted as saying that, "In 1836 he discovered and christened St. Mary's Lake." In this article, there was no mention of the cross, a priest, or the Kootenai.

Monroe died a few weeks later, and his obituary printed December 16, 1892, in the Choteau *Montanian* contained this brief reference to the St. Mary incident: "In 1836 with a party of Kootenai, he discovered and christened St. Mary's Lake, erecting a large cross there at the time." Again, no priest is mentioned.

Evaluation of Monroe's Story

The reports by Grinnell and the Montana newspapers, based on information supplied by Monroe and largely consistent with one another, offer persuasive evidence that no priest took part in the St. Mary christening ceremony. But they also bring to mind an interesting question: Why did Monroe never mention the christening publicly until the final three years of his life? The answer probably is that Monroe was never interviewed for publication before 1890, and so he was never asked about the incident. While the name of St. Mary for the lakes had been in use in some parts of Montana, such as Fort Benton, as early as 1880, no one seems to have taken an interest in learning where the name came from.

The most puzzling part of Monroe's story to the news-papers is his assertion that 1836 was the date of the ceremony at the lake. There are at least two reasons to question this state-ment, assuming he was correctly quoted: (1) The date conflicts with the one given by Grinnell, and (2) Monroe was not in Montana in 1836; Hudson's Bay Company records indicate he was employed in Canada from 1832 to 1844. Father DeSmet certainly could not have participated in 1836, since he was in Montana between 1840 and 1846, and 1845 is the year he crossed the mountains in search of the Blackfeet.

Schultz Writes About the St. Mary Christening

For almost 15 years after Monroe's death and the publication of his obituary, no public mention was made of the St. Mary incident. Then came the publication by Schultz of *My Life as an Indian*, in serial form in 1906 and in book form a year later. This work contained the first mention of a priest at the St. Mary ceremony. It asserted that "The headwaters of the South Saskatchewan were one of his (Monroe's) favorite hunting grounds. Thither in the early fifties he guided the noted Jesuit, Father DeSmet, and at the foot of the beautiful lakes lying just south of Chief Mountain they erected a huge wooden cross and named the two bodies of water St. Mary's Lakes."

So, 80 years ago, the controversy began. To confuse matters more, Schultz sometimes identified the priest in his books as Father DeSmet and sometimes as Father Lacombe. In fact, Schultz gave a somewhat different version of the christening in each of the six books in which he mentioned it. These variations are shown in the following chart:

Name of Book	Name of Priest	Date of Event
My Life as an Indian (1906–07)	DeSmet	"in the early eighteen-fifties"
Blackfeet Tales of Glacier (1916)	DeSmet	"in the 1830s"
Friends of My Life as an Indian (1923)	"a Black robe"	no date given
William Jackson, Indian Scout (1926)	Lacombe	no date given
Signposts of Adventure (1926)	Lacombe	"in the eighteen fifties"
Blackfeet and Buffalo (1962)	Lacombe	1846

None of Schultz's books was published earlier than 15 years after Monroe's death; the last was written nearly 50 years later, although it was not published until 1962. Thus, Schultz not only did not have a living Monroe to contradict him, but he had plenty of time for his memory to fade. The fertile imagination that served him so well as a storyteller was not an asset in respect to dates and other historical data, and he was not above embellishing a story to make it more colorful or believable.

DeSmet's Own Story

Father DeSmet's book, *Oregon Missions and Travels Over the Rocky Mountains, 1845–1846,* describes his extensive travels throughout the Northwest in some detail, but it contains no words about Monroe, the St. Mary lakes, or a christening ceremony. What evidence is there, then, to connect him with the incident in which Schultz says he (or another priest) participated? Surprisingly, there is other documentation which throws new light upon Father DeSmet's part in the St. Mary riddle.

Father DeSmet had become convinced by 1845 that the most pressing problem for his Flathead and Kootenai charges was the endless warfare waged against them by their aggressive and intransigent enemies, the Blackfeet. On August 1, 1845, he embarked upon a one-man crusade to visit as many of the Northwest tribes as possible. He particularly wanted to cross the Rockies, find the belligerent Blackfeet, and make peace with them, if possible.

According to his book, Father DeSmet stopped first with the Kootenai Indians, just in time to witness their annual fish festival. While in their midst, he celebrated the feast of the Assumption of the Blessed Virgin and sang a mass. He also tried a new and dramatic means of arousing their religious fervor: He erected a huge cross of pine trees on the shore of a lake. This symbol of the Christian faith had an extraordinary effect on the Indians, and he baptized a hundred adults and children.

A few days later, Father DeSmet arrived at the Prairie de Tabac, the usual abode of the Kootenai. There he found about 30 lodges of Indians camped in a large and delightful valley. He had another huge pine tree cross erected and sang a high mass before it to celebrate the feast of the Holy Heart of Mary. Again, the Indians went wild over the cross. The tribal chiefs, at the head of their people, advanced and prostrated themselves. One hundred and five people were baptized, and three of the tribesmen, upon learning where he was going, volunteered to escort the priest over the mountains.

Father DeSmet left the Kootenai camp August 30, and toward noon of September 4 he found himself at the headwaters of the Columbia River. There he visited for a few days with a Canadian trapper named Morigeau and his family. Despite the lack of a multitude, DeSmet erected on the plain another huge cross and celebrated a mass on the occasion of the Feast of the Nativity of the Blessed Virgin. Under the cross, he baptized the wife and children of Morigeau, and he declared that the plain where the cross stood should thereafter be called the Plain of the Nativity.

Bidding goodbye September 9 to the Morigeaus, Father DeSmet and his trio of protectors crossed the valleys of the Kootenai and Vermillion Rivers and "traversed the highlands separating the waters of Oregon from those of the south branch of the Saskatchewan." On the shore of a beautiful lake, now thought to have been Lake Louise, he erected still another huge cross, and he called it the "Cross of Peace" in honor of his mission to the Blackfeet. He was probably pleased with the remarkable results produced by his series of crosses, and he marveled at the way a rustic cross seemed able to transform the wilderness into a shrine or temple.

After resting a few days, Father DeSmet and his companions pressed on in a northeasterly direction. They arrived at

Rocky Mountain House, a Hudson's Bay Company post, on October 4 and enjoyed the hospitality of the post factor, J. E. Harriote. On October 25, a band of 13 Blackfeet arrived at the post. They cordially invited DeSmet to travel with them southward or to let them be his guide.

However, Father DeSmet elected to travel on his own. He left Rocky Mountain House October 31 accompanied by a young Cree to handle the horses and a half-breed interpreter and guide named Bird. On the twelfth day out, the interpreter disappeared. A trapper the priest encountered recommended a Canadian interpreter who lived farther along the route Father DeSmet was traveling, so he decided to keep going. (Could Monroe have been the Canadian interpreter? Hudson's Bay Company records indicate he was employed as an interpreter in Canada from 1832 to 1844.)

The priest and the young Cree struggled southward for another eight days, including four on which it snowed. Having found neither the Canadian interpreter nor the Blackfeet, they had no alternative but to return to one of the Hudson's Bay Company posts to the north. They found their way back to Fort Edmonton, arriving "toward the close of the year."

Additional Light on the Journey

If Father DeSmet had left no more information than the published story of his 1845–46 travels, there would be little evidence to connect him with the christening of the St. Mary lakes. However, in a letter dated June 13, 1850, the priest wrote to Hugh Monroe:

> *I cannot let Mr. Harvey start without giving you a sign of life and some little news of myself. Though I have never had the good fortune to see you, I have heard your name often, and I have always heard you so well*

spoken of that I have for years past considered you a dear and personally familiar friend. Mr. Harvey has been kind enough to come and see me; he had told me a great deal about you and I have listened with the greatest pleasure. Ah! How much I regret that I was so hindered by circumstances, and that I did not meet you on my first visit to the Blackfeet territory. I traveled through a labyrinth of narrow valleys on the eastern slope of the Rocky Mountains, and plains that seemed endless—always searching for you—I looked forward to doing immense good among the savages, through you. I followed your traces to your encampment at the foot of the Quilloux mountain, where I found the signs that you had left, evidently for my benefit—then I took up your trail with fresh courage, believing you to be very near; later a little misunderstanding on the part of my guides caused me to lose them, and we began wandering as chance might lead to the point of discouragement. Then snow began to fall in great flakes and to cover the ground with a thick layer—and with it vanished my hope of finding you, that season, in some Blackfeet camp. So, I deferred my visit to the following summer, and made my way in haste back to the plains, where the snow was not so deep and so to Fort Augustus on the Saskatchewan. There again I expected you, but in vain, for two months. The worthy and respectable Messrs Rowan and Harriote, at this post, were very attentive to me, and I shall always be grateful to them.

Another bit of information about Father DeSmet's travels east of the mountains in 1845 can be found on a map in his book on the Oregon missions (see page 31). It indicates that, in his southward trek, he did not reach or cross the boundary between Canadian and U.S. territory. This appears to be incorrect for two reasons: (1) Since he found Monroe's encampment, he had to be south of the border; and (2) since his round-trip from Rocky Mountain House at Fort Edmonton covered a distance of 600 hundred miles in 40 days (assuming a return to Fort Edmonton by December 10), the 20 days he spent traveling southward would have taken him 300 miles south of Rocky Mountain House—far enough to have brought him well south of the border.

Three Keys to a Solution

There appears to be no question that Monroe named the lakes in the 1840s in the company of a huge cross of pine and a party of Kootenai Indians. But the story prompts many other questions. Why would a lay person perform a christening ceremony, a rite usually reserved for clergy? Why were the Indians gathered together for the ceremony? Why a pine cross? And why the name St. Mary?

If one studies all the facts available, there appear to be three keys to the solution of the mystery: (1) The unusual series of pine tree crosses raised by Father DeSmet while en route to the east side of the mountains; (2) the letter written by Father DeSmet to Monroe, relating the priest's unsuccessful attempt to find the Canadian; and (3) the unusual relationship between Monroe and the Kootenais.

One possible theory is that Monroe was urged by a group of visiting Indians to erect a cross and emulate a ceremony they had witnessed earlier at their own camp.

It is plausible that the Kootenais, having witnessed the raising of a wooden cross by Father DeSmet at their camp in the summer of 1845, would hasten over the mountains to visit their Catholic friend, Monroe, and beg him to erect a similar cross and perform what appeared to be a similar ceremony.

Otherwise, how would Monroe have known of the crosses being raised elsewhere by Father DeSmet?

There is nothing in the very complete biography of his life by Chittenden and Richardson to suggest that Father DeSmet ever made use of this dramatic device at any time in his missionary career other than on the four occasions mentioned in his book.

The raising of a huge cross at Monroe's camp, several hundred miles from the sites of Father DeSmet's crosses, had to be more than mere coincidence. Someone who had witnessed one of Father DeSmet's ceremonies had to have suggested the idea to Monroe. The only individuals who could have done so were the Kootenais, who were Catholics and friends of Monroe, who had witnessed such a ceremony, and who knew the way over the mountains to Monroe's customary encampment.

The letter Father DeSmet wrote to Monroe in 1850 holds the second key to the mystery. It indicates that Monroe was the interpreter for whom the priest searched in November 1845, and it reveals that Father DeSmet actually found Monroe's abandoned camp. Finally, it states that when the priest reached the camp, he saw something he assumed was left for his benefit. That something, in all probability, was the huge cross Monroe had erected on the shore of the lake during the christening ceremony a few weeks earlier.

Whatever it was, Father DeSmet was so impressed by what he had seen that he wrote a letter to a man he had never met. His letter rules him out as having any direct connection with the christening. Thus, it tends to reinforce Monroe's own story that only Kootenai Indians were present at the ceremony.

The third key and, in some respects, the most important, was the unusual relationship between Monroe and the Kootenai tribe. Although Monroe had close ties with the Blackfeet, the Kootenais were fellow Catholics and his closest friends.

More than 20 years earlier, he had persuaded them to trade their furs with the Hudson's Bay Company, and they dearly loved this white man, whom they could visit simply by slipping over one of the passes that led to Monroe's back door.

A visit by the Kootenais in 1845 was probably directly responsible for the christening. They may have been eager to share with Monroe the spiritual elation they had experienced when Father DeSmet raised a pine-tree cross in their own camp, and to induce him to repeat this novel and thrilling incident for their benefit. For Monroe, it was an opportunity to make his friends happy not only by honoring their idol, Father DeSmet, the founder of the St. Mary Mission west of the mountains, but by conferring upon the lakes a name that was very dear to them.

Some Interesting Answers

This theory supplies logical answers to the principal questions heretofore posed:

Did a Catholic priest participate in the christening?

The answer is no! The ceremony was conducted by Monroe alone, at the request and for the benefit of his Kootenai friends.

What was Father DeSmet's role?

His role was indirect and minor. He almost certainly inspired the erection of the cross of logs, and his beloved St. Mary Mission probably inspired the name for the lakes. This suggests that the priest was in the area about the time of the christening. The fact that he seems to have seen the St. Mary cross indicates he came shortly after the ceremony.

When did the christening take place?

The St. Mary cross was most likely erected in September or October 1845, a period which saw the erection of four similar crosses by Father DeSmet in relatively adjacent mountain territory.

The fact that Father DeSmet visited Monroe's camp in 1845 and saw signs evidently left for his benefit leaves little room for doubt that it was also 1845 when Monroe and his Kootenai friends erected a cross of their own during a formal christening ceremony.

More and Different Evidence

Just when the evidence seems to prove conclusively that the St. Mary lakes were named in 1845, there comes to light an entirely different story. It is contained in a memoir by Henry A. Kennerly, who was an eyewitness to the 1855 treaty council between federal commissioners and Indians of the Northwest. Kennerly was 19 at the time of the events described in his memoir, which was prepared only a few months before his death in 1913.

Kennerly explained that he was sent, with Baptiste Champine as guide and interpreter, to visit the Blackfeet tribes in Canada and to notify them of the time and place of the forthcoming treaty council meeting. He delivered his message to Chief Lame Bull and his followers, and Lame Bull sent messengers to the tribes farther north. Kennerly and his guide then turned south to Fort Benton. From the memoir is taken the following report of pertinent events:

> *Shortly after leaving Lame Bull's camp, we discovered quite a large party of people traveling in a southerly direction and, being curious to know who they were, started in pursuit. We overtook them near Chief Mountain and found it to be a party of half-breeds and Indians that were accompanying Father LaCom, a Catholic missionary priest. [We] were invited by the Father to join his party and to travel with them as long as our path was in the same direction.*

We accepted the invitation and that evening camped on the shores of a beautiful lake situated in a deep gorge of the mountains, from which a large and sparkling stream of water flowed that was alive with trout and other species of large fish. This lake at that time had no English name applied to it and it was known only by the Indian name of "Paukt-to-muo-kima," the meaning of which is "Lakes under the Bluff," while the stream flowing from the lakes was called "Ats-ski-Kix," the meaning of which is "blue banks." In all probability Father LaCom and myself were the first white men that ever camped on the shores of this lake.

While we were here encamped, Father LaCom caused to be constructed a large cross of pine logs and, planting it firmly in the ground on the shores of this lake, and after going through the usual ceremonies customary with the Catholics upon such occasions, baptized and christened this beautiful body of water to the name of "Lake St. Mary" and the stream to be known as the "St. Mary River."

At the time the naming of the lake took place, Father LaCom was under the impression that it was north of the International Boundary Line and within Her Majesty's Domain. Subsequent observations and surveys by competent engineers, however, located it about 10 miles south of the boundary line and within the territory of the United States. While I am now on the subject of the lakes, I will make the prediction that, at no distant day, St. Mary Lakes will become a popular resort to tourists and others that are visiting the Glacier National Park.

After bidding farewell to Father LaCom and members of his party, Baptiste and I resumed our journey towards Fort Benton.[2]

Apparently, the priest and his half-breeds never told of the christening, as this version of the story escapes notice elsewhere in Montana history. The only thing that lends it any credibility is that Henry Kennerly, a nephew of William Clark of the Lewis and Clark expedition, was a man of probity. He later served as treasurer of Chouteau County and was a member of the Montana Legislature.

Yet, Kennerly doesn't seem to have mentioned the event in the 57 years between it and the publication of his memoirs. One wonders how anyone learned prior to 1913 that the lakes had been named St. Mary.

On the other hand, Monroe, after christening the lakes, continued to live in their vicinity for the remainder of his life, and he mentioned his 1845 ceremony to several writers. By the time Kennerly wrote his memoir, the story of Monroe's ceremony would have appeared in several Montana newspapers to which Kennerly would have had access. And Monroe, who had died years earlier, was not around to contradict anything Kennerly had to say.

In Kennerly's story, the identification of those present at the christening is vague. He makes no mention of who the half-breeds were or where they were going. Kennerly identifies the priest as Father LaCom, apparently referring to the well-known Canadian Black Robe, Father Albert Lacombe. However, Father Lacombe's biography shows he was nowhere near the international border in 1855 and, in fact, was never south of it until 1869.

The event of 1855, if it ever occurred, had no motivational background. Its performance was without purpose or reason, while the contrary was true of the 1845 ceremony conducted by Monroe. When Monroe named the lakes, there were special and unique reasons for erecting a log cross and honoring the name of St. Mary.

In any event, the incident of 1855 cannot possibly have any bearing on the 1845 christening. Even if the later event took place, it still does nothing to disprove the 1845 christening or the story told by Monroe to such a reliable reporter as George Bird Grinnell.

Regardless of whether the lakes were christened once or twice, and whatever the verdict of history in the matter, two things are certain: The name given the lakes was St. Mary, and they are undoubtedly the only lakes in the world formally christened beneath a huge cross of pine logs.

3

Father DeSmet

Super-Missionary

The inexhaustible Catholic priest Father Pierre Jean DeSmet traveled thousands of miles around the world in his efforts to bring peace and Christianity to the Indians of the American Northwest. Some believe he presided over the christening of the St. Mary lakes, though evidence exists to the contrary. *Courtesy of Montana Historical Society*

Pierre Jean DeSmet was born January 30, 1801, in the village of Termonde, Belgium, along with his twin sister, Coleta Aldegunda. His family was one of the most respectable in Belgium, and young DeSmet came into the world assured of a comfortable beginning to life. His father was Josse Arnaud DeSmet, and his mother was Josse Arnaud's second wife, Marie Jeanne Buydens. The couple had nine children; Pierre Jean was the fifth.

Pierre Jean was a healthy, handsome child. In school, he was a distinguished pupil, exhibiting the tact and common sense that would serve him well later in life. He was noted for his extraordinary physical strength and his skill at sports. So prominent were these abilities that his classmates nicknamed him Samson.

Pierre Jean's early years were spent at his parents' home, but when he became old enough to begin serious study, he was sent to the Seminary of Malines, where he remained until his 21st year.

While at the seminary, DeSmet decided to pursue a religious life and to become a missionary. Not unnaturally, he was attracted to the Catholic order whose principal purpose was missionary work—the Society of Jesus, or Jesuits. When a zealous missionary from the New World who had returned to Belgium in search of funds and recruits painted a vivid picture of the need for workers in America, his fervent appeal aroused the enthusiasm of students at Malines. Six of them, including DeSmet, volunteered to go.

After a 40-day voyage across the Atlantic on the brig *Columbus,* the little band found itself in Philadelphia. The missionaries visited Baltimore, Washington, D.C., and Georgetown and entered the Jesuit novitiate at Whitemarsh to commence their long career as novices. After six years there, Father DeSmet was ordained a priest, and on April 11, 1823, he joined a group heading to St. Louis to establish a second novitiate. Traveling on foot—except for an interlude when they journeyed by raft on the Ohio River from Wheeling, West Virginia, to Shawneetown, Illinois—they arrived at St. Louis on the last day of May. They continued another 15 miles to the little village of Florissant, where they founded the second novitiate of the Society of Jesus in the United States.

When their efforts to establish schools for Indian children failed, they resolved to establish an institute of learning in St. Louis. The college, founded there in the fall of 1829, is today St. Louis University, and Father DeSmet was a member of the original faculty. In 1834, the Vatican approved a proposal that the Jesuits teach the Catholic religion to the Omaha, Pawnee, Arikara, Sioux, Mandan, Assiniboine, Crow, Blackfeet, Shoshone, and Flathead tribes.

Many of the tribes in the Northwest, including the Flathead, had heard of the "Black Robes" from the Iroquois, who had already embraced Catholicism while living in eastern Canada and who had migrated into the Northwest searching for furs. The Flatheads wanted to learn from the Black Robes, too. So in 1831 they sent a deputation to St. Louis to ask that a priest visit them. The mission failed, and deputations were sent again in 1835, 1837, and 1839. Finally, on the fourth try, the bishop promised to send a priest the following spring.

Father DeSmet volunteered for the job. In 1840, he left St. Louis by steamboat for Westport (Kansas City) and there joined the annual expedition of the American Fur Company to the mountains. The party left Westport April 30, following the general route of the Oregon Trail, and it reached the annual rendezvous on Green River two months later. During this trip, Father DeSmet suffered an attack of malaria, which lingered on for several months.

The priest was met at Green River by a deputation of 10 Flathead Indians. On Sunday, Father DeSmet celebrated the first formal mass on the prairie—the first ceremony of its kind in the Rocky Mountains north of the Mexican possessions.

From Green River, Father DeSmet and the Flatheads traveled to the main camp of the tribe at Pierre's Hole, where 1,600

Indians waited to greet him. He was surprised to find the wild tribes of the mountains completely absorbed in fervent religious teaching. Eventually, the entire party marched to Flathead country, ascending Henry Fork of the Snake River and arriving at Henry Lake July 22. During the next month, DeSmet and his Indian friends traveled leisurely down to the valley of the Jefferson River and from there to the Three Forks on the Missouri.

Convinced that a permanent mission should be established, Father DeSmet decided to return home and seek permission to build one. He followed a route which closely paralleled the modern line of the Northern Pacific Railroad, striking the Yellowstone River where Livingston, Montana, now stands. He followed the Yellowstone to Fort Union, left there September 23, and traveled on foot to Fort Clark, Fort Pierre, and Fort Vermillion. There, he commissioned a canoe to take him to St. Joseph Mission at Council Bluffs. He arrived in St. Louis on the last day of the year.

Father DeSmet was disappointed to learn that no money was available for his mission. Undaunted, he went to New Orleans and in a few weeks raised the amount he needed for his project on his own. Accompanied by three priests and three lay brothers, he left St. Louis for the West the following spring. They reached Fort Hall on the Snake River about the middle of August, where they met an advance guard of the Flatheads. They reached the Deer Lodge Valley early in September, having been joined en route by the main Flathead camp, and they continued on to the Bitterroot Valley, some 30 miles from modern Missoula, Montana, near present-day Stevensville, Montana. There they chose the site of their first establishment, to be called St. Mary's Mission. They started work on its construction September 24, 1841.

Father DeSmet and his party, assisted by the Indians, worked industriously through the winter of 1841–42. With the approach of spring, the priest decided to visit the lower Columbia River for additional supplies, as well as to visit with the new missionary there and with the governor of the Hudson's Bay Company at Fort Vancouver. He left St. Mary's early in April, traveled to Fort Colville, and arrived at Fort Vancouver June 8, 1842. There, to his great pleasure, he met Fathers Modeste Demers and Francis Blanchet, who had arrived two years before. He visited their mission on the Willamette River, and among them they decided he should go to Europe to seek recruits and funds.

Father DeSmet returned to St. Mary's, where he told his brethren and the Indians of his plans and promised to return. After spending two weeks at Three Forks with the Flatheads who were there on a buffalo hunt, he set out eastward August 15 for St. Louis by way of Fort Union and the Missouri River.

Early in 1843, Father DeSmet went as far south as New Orleans and as far east as Boston in search of funds and recruits. He succeeded in securing financial assistance, as well as in recruiting two priests and a lay brother. Immediately after returning to St. Louis, he set out for Europe. After a voyage of 21 days, he landed in Ireland and then traveled to the principal cities of England, France, Italy, Holland, and Belgium, seeking aid for his missions. In Rome, when Father DeSmet was presented to Pope Gregory XVI by the Father General of the Society of Jesus, the pontiff rose from his throne and embraced him. When Father DeSmet learned that he was to be made a bishop, he asked the Father General to help get the honor transferred to Father Blanchet instead.

On December 12, 1843, Father DeSmet embarked at Antwerp on the *Indefatigable* together with four fathers, six sisters, a lay brother, and a large amount of supplies for the missions. They were detained at Flushing, near the mouth of the Scheld River, by contrary winds for 28 days, and they did not actually get under way until January 9, 1844.

Part of the voyage was unpleasant, for the ship encountered a succession of terrific storms after rounding Cape Horn. Stops at Valparaiso, Chile, and Callao, Peru, gave the passengers a chance to spend time on shore. They left Callao May 27 and, despite being becalmed for a time, arrived at the mouth of the Columbia River on the Oregon coast July 28. Another three days were needed to get the *Indefatigable* over the dangerous bar at the mouth of the great river.

Father DeSmet contacted the new bishop, Blanchet, and they headed for the Willamette Valley to choose a site for the central mission, which had been approved in Rome. While construction was under way, Father DeSmet became dangerously ill for a time. Still, he departed October 3 for Flathead country. Because of various delays, he only got as far as the new Sacred Heart Mission among the Coeur d' Alene Indians when the onset of winter prevented further progress. He returned to spend the winter with some friendly Indians about 40 miles above the mouth of the Columbia.

Early in February 1845, while snow was yet deep on the ground, Father DeSmet started for St. Mary's, thinking he could make the journey and return before the spring melt began. He succeeded and, after helping to start the new buildings for a mission promised to the Kalispels, he went to Fort Vancouver and the Willamette for more supplies. With 11 horses laden with implements and provisions, he soon started back north, on his way establishing two new stations—one at Kettle Falls and the other at Lake de Boey.

As summer approached, Father DeSmet realized there would never be peace among the Indian tribes unless a means of pacifying the truculent Blackfeet could be found. They were even endangering the continued existence of St. Mary's

Mission. The priest decided to visit the Blackfeet on the east side of the Rockies and try to check their warlike behavior.

Instead of heading straight east across the mountains, Father DeSmet elected to travel a hundred miles north before turning east. In that way, he expected to be able to visit more Indian tribes en route. He set forth about August 1, 1845, and he arrived among the Kootenai Indians in time to witness their annual fish festival. Also while there, he celebrated the feast of the Assumption of the Blessed Virgin Mary, at which he sang a mass and baptized 100 adults and children. Here also, on the shore of a lake, he erected the first of several crosses to be raised in the course of his trans-mountain journey.

Then Father DeSmet traveled for a few days to the Prairie du Tabac, the usual abode of the Kootenais. There he found about 30 lodges of Indians in a camp situated in an immense and delightful valley. While visiting with them, he sang a high mass to celebrate the feast of the Holy Heart of Mary and baptized 105 people. A large cross was erected before which the tribal chiefs, at the head of their people, prostrated themselves. Three Kootenais volunteered to escort the priest across the mountains.

Father DeSmet left the Kootenais August 30 and, toward noon September 4, found himself at two small lakes which were the source of the Columbia River. Here, he met a Canadian trapper and hunter named Morigeau and his wife and family. Originally from St. Martin near Montreal, Canada, Morigeau had lived near the head of the Columbia for 26 years. While with the Morigeaus, Father DeSmet baptized the wife and children and celebrated a mass of the Nativity of the Blessed Virgin. A large cross was erected on the plain, which was thereafter called the Plain of the Nativity.

Bidding goodbye September 9 to the Morigeau family, Father DeSmet and his escort of three Kootenais crossed the valleys of the Kootenai and Vermillion Rivers and traversed the Continental Divide. Once again, on the bank of what is thought to have been Lake Louise, he raised the Christian standard, the cross, in the hope, he later wrote, that "it might be a sign of salvation and peace to the scattered and itinerant tribes east and west of these gigantic and lurid mountains."

On October 4, 1845, Father DeSmet arrived at Rocky Mountain House, a prominent trading post of the Hudson's Bay Company, built in 1805 by Simon Fraser at the eastern end of what was called the Rocky Mountain Portage. The fort commander was J. E. Harriote. On October 25, a band of 13 Blackfeet arrived and visited amiably with Father DeSmet, even inviting him to their territory and offering to be his guides. The priest did not accept the invitation and elected to head south to Blackfeet country on his own. He arranged to travel with a young Cree who would handle the horses, and a half-breed interpreter named Bird, whom he had been warned not to trust.

They left Rocky Mountain House October 31, and after nine days on the trail, during which the priest had many misgivings about the interpreter, they encountered a Canadian and his Indian family and persuaded them to join the party. The following day, the interpreter disappeared. The Canadian advised the priest that he might find a Canadian interpreter named Monroe some distance ahead. So Father DeSmet and his young helper continued southward, wandering for eight days in a "labyrinth of valleys, but in vain." Although they traveled through the heart of Blackfeet territory, the pair found neither the Canadian nor any Blackfeet. Their supply of food was low, their horses were nearly exhausted, winter was upon them, and to return west across the mountains was impractical. Father DeSmet realized they had no alternative but to return to one of the Hudson's Bay Company forts and ask for hospitality for the winter.

According to his correspondence, the priest returned to Fort Augustus, or Edmonton, arriving "toward the close of the year." The post commander, John Rowan, gave him a warm welcome.

The map included in *Oregon Missions and Travels Over the Rocky Mountains,* written by Father DeSmet and published in 1847, indicates that he never traveled as far south as the U.S.–Canadian border. This must be incorrect for two reasons: Father DeSmet's letter of June 12, 1850, to Hugh Monroe indicates that he found the latter's camp, which must have been at Lower St. Mary Lake, well south of the border. Also, if December 10 is assumed to be the date the priest returned to Fort Edmonton, he spent a total of 40 days traveling round-trip. At normal rates of horseback travel on the Canadian plains, the 20 days spent marching south would have taken him 300 miles— far enough below Rocky Mountain House to bring him well south of the border.

As soon as spring approached and he had a chance of getting back across the mountains, Father DeSmet headed by dogsled for Fort Assiniboine and then to Fort Jasper, where he remained until April 25. He then set forth on the hazardous trip across the mountains. Despite numerous delays, the little party made its way over a pass to the point called Boat Encampment, where the Canoe River enters the Columbia. He made it to Fort Colville near the end of May and then to Fort Vancouver and the Willamette Valley.

As the number of missions had grown, so had the need for more aid from the states and Europe. So the Jesuit missionaries agreed unanimously that Father DeSmet should travel east once more. Outfitting himself with supplies, he set out from Fort Vancouver to visit the outposts farther north and then to return to the states. He arrived at St. Mary's Mission August 10 and left on the 16th. Since his peacemaking mission to the

Blackfeet had failed the previous autumn, he decided to try again as he traveled.

In the next month, a large party of Crows attacked a camp made up mostly of Flatheads, as well as 30 lodges of Nez Perce and a few lodges of Blackfeet. The Crows were repulsed with heavy losses. When Father DeSmet arrived at the camp shortly thereafter, the Blackfeet came to his lodge to express their admiration for the Flatheads. As the allied camp set forth for Fort Lewis (later renamed Fort Benton), a truce was forged between Blackfeet and Flatheads, and the growing admiration of the Blackfeet for the priest and his religion paved the way for the founding of a mission with this fierce tribe.

Father DeSmet left Fort Lewis September 28, traveling by skiff on the long journey of 2,200 miles to St. Louis. At Council Bluffs, he found 10,000 Mormons camped and ready to head west in search of a new home. They asked the priest many questions about the regions he had explored, and they were pleased with the account he gave them of the Great Salt Lake basin. Father DeSmet reached St. Louis December 10, 1846.

In the previous seven years, Father DeSmet had traveled a distance more than twice the Earth's circumference. He had traveled in almost every climate, from the burning summer of the equator to the freezing winter of Canada. He had traveled by sailing vessel, by river barge and canoe, by dogsled and snowshoe, on horseback and in wagon, and many a long mile on foot. He had endured hardships that likely contributed to the ill health he would suffer later in life.

In a letter to a fellow missionary who had complained about his lot, Father DeSmet referred to the years 1844–46 like this:

I have for years been a wanderer in the desert. I was three years without receiving a letter from any quarter.

I was two years in the mountains without tasting bread, salt, coffee, tea, sugar. I was for years without a roof, without a bed. I have been six months without a shirt on my back, and often I have passed whole days and nights without a morsel of anything to eat.

The results of Father DeSmet's labors were, in the view of his church, highly successful. The whole Columbia Valley was dotted with infant missions, some of which promised to become permanent. He had laid the foundation for a spiritual empire.

Perhaps most important, however, was the fact that he had gained great influence among the Indian tribes. All now knew him—many personally, the rest by reputation. He was the one white in whom they had implicit faith. The U.S. government was beginning to look to him for assistance. The Mormon, the "forty-niner," and the Oregon settler came to him for information and advice. His writings were already known on two continents, and his name was a familiar one, at least in the religious world.

Although Father DeSmet repeatedly asked to return to missionary work, his superiors instead named him procurator of the Prince in St. Louis, an office which related to the financial affairs of the Catholic Church. His great ability in securing contributions made him admirably fitted for this work, but it was personally distasteful to him.

The main reason Father DeSmet was not permitted to conduct further missions was a growing feeling in Rome that he was planning on too large a scale. The Father General had been told that Father DeSmet's descriptions of his work were exaggerated. The priest was deeply hurt by these accusations, and he vigorously defended himself. Nevertheless, his missionary days were over.

The year after his return to St. Louis in 1846, Father DeSmet journeyed to Europe, returning to America in midsummer 1848. The years 1849 and 1850 were spent in St. Louis, except for several occasions on which he visited Catholic institutions around the country.

The great rush of people to Oregon and California in the 1840s wrought a profound change on the West. The Indian, seeing his once undisputed domain slipping steadily from his grasp, grew restless and discontented. To avoid trouble, the U.S. government proposed holding a general council of all the tribes east of the Rocky Mountains, in hopes of reaching an understanding with them.

The council was held in 1851, and Father DeSmet was asked by the government to participate. This would be the beginning of a new role for the priest; he would serve as peacemaker for the United States for the rest of his life.

Father DeSmet left St. Louis June 7, 1851, on the steamboat *St. Ange,* and arrived at Fort Union July 14. There, he prepared for the journey overland to Fort Laramie, where the great council would be held.

On July 31, Father DeSmet and a party of 32 whites and Indians began the trek southward over the plains of eastern Montana to a point near the present town of Casper, Wyoming. Then they turned eastward to Fort Laramie and the valley of Horse Creek, where government representatives and 10,000 Indians were gathered. The council lasted September 12–23, and everyone seemed satisfied with what it accomplished. Father DeSmet played an important role, using his great influence to promote a satisfactory understanding. He returned overland directly to St. Louis, arriving there October 21.

The priest spent the following year fulfilling his regular duties as procurator. In the spring of 1853, he started on another trip to Europe, accompanied by Bishop John Miege.

While passing through Washington, D.C., the pair were presented to President Franklin Pierce, and Father DeSmet was asked to deliver dispatches to several European powers. He and his companion sailed May 9 on the steamer *Fulton* and crossed in 11 days—a great improvement over the 40-day crossing of 1821, which had brought the priest to America for the first time.

He left for home November 23 on the steamer *Humboldt*. The voyage was rough and slow, and the ship had to stop at Halifax, Canada, for coal. Due to the incompetence of the pilot, the vessel was wrecked and lost, but the passengers and crew were saved. After a short delay, the passengers boarded the *Niagara* and steamed to Boston. Father DeSmet was back in St. Louis December 26.

The priest spent 1854, 1855, and most of 1856 in St. Louis, except for some brief journeys to the various Catholic establishments in the Mississippi Valley. In September 1856, he reluctantly made *yet* another trip to Europe, and he returned in April 1857.

For six years, the priest had not been to Indian country, but in 1858 a call for help came from an unexpected quarter. The Mormon rebellion of 1857–58 was in progress and, at first, the Mormons had gotten the better of federal troops. When a military expedition under General William Harney was ordered west, the officer asked to have Father DeSmet accompany him as chaplain. The priest left St. Louis May 20, 1858, to join the command at Fort Leavenworth.

Father DeSmet was impressed by how settled the country had become since he had last ventured across the Great Plains. He was also astonished at the long wagon trains being used to transport provisions and stores of war to Utah. General Harney's expedition made its way safely as far as the ford of the South Platte River, where word was received that peace had been restored in Utah and the expedition should turn back.

Father DeSmet arrived in St. Louis in the early part of September and tendered his resignation from the Army. It was not accepted, however, because of new trouble among the Indians in distant Oregon country. The incursion of white people onto Indian lands in the territories of Oregon and Washington had irritated the tribes. Again, the government decided to send General Harney and an expeditionary force to handle the situation, and again Harney asked Father DeSmet to accompany him. So he retained his post as chaplain and went to Oregon by way of Panama, sailing from New York September 20, 1858, and arriving at Fort Vancouver October 28. Again, the uprising had ended before General Harney arrived.

However, the Indians still needed soothing, and Father DeSmet was asked to visit the northern tribes to seek peace. He left Fort Vancouver October 29 and spent the winter among the Coeur d'Alenes at the Sacred Heart Mission. On February 18, 1859, he set out for Flathead country and visited the site of the abandoned St. Mary's Mission and the new mission of St. Ignatius near Flathead Lake.

On April 16, under orders from General Harney, Father DeSmet left St. Ignatius with the chiefs of the various mountain tribes to take them to Fort Vancouver, where they were to confer with government officers. They arrived at Fort Vancouver May 18, 1859, and the council was held the next day with satisfactory results. Feeling that he could be of no further service, Father DeSmet asked permission to return to the states by way of the mountain missions and the Missouri River. With General Harney's permission, he left Fort Vancouver June 15 and traveled east by way of St. Ignatius, the Mullan Road, and Great Falls to Fort Benton. He left the fort August 5 with a skiff and oarsman, safely navigating to Omaha, where he boarded a steamboat to St. Louis.

Some idea of the priest's zeal may be inferred from the fact that on this journey he baptized about 900 Indian children. Along the Missouri he met many tribes, always stopping a day or two to give them religious instruction. They invariably showed him great respect and affection and listened to his words with the utmost attention.

Father DeSmet remained in St. Louis, except for some short side trips, until September 1860, when he again set out for Europe. He confined his travels on the continent to France, Belgium, and Holland, and on April 2, 1861, he returned home aboard the *Fulton,* learning upon his arrival in New York of the fall of Fort Sumter in South Carolina. Throughout the Civil War, his prayers were for peace, but his sympathies were with the North.

Father DeSmet made three trips to Washington, D.C., during 1861 and 1862. He had the honor of talking with President Abraham Lincoln for more than an hour, and of dining with the ambassadors of Belgium, France, Russia, and Spain. In the summer of 1862, he made the long journey to Fort Benton and back, traveling on the American Fur Company steamboat *Spread Eagle.* While at Fort Benton, he visited the great falls of the Missouri, which would later be the site of the city of Great Falls, Montana.

The war between the United States and the Sioux Indians in 1862 and 1863 greatly interfered with Father DeSmet's plans. He had hoped to start a mission among the Sioux in 1863, but he had to abandon the attempt for a time. He did make another trip to Fort Benton, leaving St. Louis May 9, 1863, with two Italian brothers on the American Fur Company steamboat *Nellie Rogers.* The passengers were stranded by low water for several weeks at the mouth of the Milk River. During this interlude, a half-breed was murdered, and Father DeSmet prevented a nearby band of Indians from seeking revenge.

Unable to travel down the Missouri, Father DeSmet decided to return to St. Louis via the Pacific Ocean. He left Fort Benton for St. Ignatius Mission August 25 and reached Fort Vancouver October 8. He sailed from Portland to San Francisco, and from there to the Isthmus of Panama, arriving in New York on Thanksgiving Day. He finally reached St. Louis December 1.

In 1864, there was great unrest among the Sioux tribes of the Dakota Territory, and the U.S. government asked Father DeSmet to act again as peacemaker. He headed up the Missouri River on the steamboat *Yellowstone,* which moved slowly because of river conditions. He reached Fort Berthold, more than 1,900 miles above St. Louis, June 9. Nearby were camped the Mandans, Gros Ventres, and Arikaras, banded together for mutual protection against the Sioux. The three tribes received the priest with great cordiality. He told them of his plan to contact the Sioux with a message of peace from President Lincoln, and he sent a messenger to the Sioux, asking to meet with them.

On July 8, to the dismay and terror of the three tribes, a formidable body of Sioux warriors appeared on the opposite bank of the Missouri. Contrary to the advice of the whites at the fort and the impassioned pleas of his Indians friends, Father DeSmet paddled across the river in a small skiff to meet with the Sioux, who greeted him with tokens of friendship and respect.

The meeting lasted three hours, and when he returned to his anxious friends on the west bank, he was able to reassure them that the Sioux had not come to attack them, but rather to hear the message the Black Robe had brought.

It is doubtful any other white man—fur hunter, Indian trader, soldier, government agent, priest, or settler—could have crossed the Missouri River at Fort Berthold that July day and survived.

Late in August 1864, Father DeSmet went to Washington, D.C., to give a report of his trip. A week after his return to St. Louis, he sailed for Europe, spending time in England, Belgium, and Italy. In Rome, he was again received with great consideration by Pope Gregory XVI. He returned to Belgium in December and spent the first part of 1865 visiting the principal cities of that country and of Holland, England, and Ireland. He sailed from Liverpool, England, June 7 and was back in St. Louis by June 30. Soon after he sailed from Europe, he was made a Chevalier of the Order of Leopold by the Belgian king.

In 1866, Father DeSmet made his last trip to Fort Benton, leaving St. Louis April 9. At Fort Sully, he met a number of Sioux Indians who confided in him about their mistreatment and sufferings at the hands of the whites. He reached Fort Benton June 7, after a prosperous voyage in which he had satisfactory interviews with all the river tribes. He was back in St. Louis by the middle of July and remained there the rest of the year.

The U.S. government by this time was at a critical point in its relations with the Indian tribes, and constant efforts were being made to make peace. The years 1867 and 1868 were the most important in Father DeSmet's life because of the part he took in this pacification. He had greater influence with the Indians than any other living white man, and the government was glad to avail itself of his services. Early in 1867, the secretary of the interior asked him to visit the hostile tribes and to convince them to make peace and submit. He accepted the commission with the understanding that he would take no remuneration for his services.

Father DeSmet left St. Louis April 12, 1867, and arrived in Fort Buford some weeks later. Thousands of Indians waited along the route to see and talk with him. He became convinced that if they were justly treated, the problems would be solved. This was undoubtedly true, but the conditions named by Father DeSmet were impossible for the government to meet. The onward rush of immigrants could not be checked, and it was this, primarily, that was causing the conflict. He spent four months on this mission and did a great deal to prepare the minds of the Indians for peace.

On March 30, 1868, Father DeSmet left St. Louis on the most important mission of his whole career. He accompanied members of the new peace commission appointed by the government to deal with the Indian problem. Among the members were Generals William Sherman, Philip Sheridan, William Harney, Alfred Terry, and several others. They went to Cheyenne and Fort Laramie while Father DeSmet went to Fort Rice.

The priest assembled a party of about 80 friendly Sioux to help him find the camp of the hostiles. They traveled a considerable distance until, near the spot where the Powder River empties into the Yellowstone, a group of scouts returned at the head of a deputation of 18 warriors who announced, after smoking the pipe of peace together, that their camp was open to the Black Robe only, that no other white men were welcome.

The main camp of the hostiles consisted of some 4,000 to 5,000 Indians under their leader, Sitting Bull. Father DeSmet was warmly received, and a large lodge had been prepared for him. After the priest had rested, Sitting Bull told him how badly his people had been treated by the whites. The priest agreed to meet with the Sioux chiefs the next day, June 20, to decide whether the Indians would see the commissioners.

Great preparations were made for the council. A circular space of about 170 feet in diameter was enclosed by a high wall of buffalo robes. The pipe of peace was smoked and Father DeSmet was invited to talk, which he did for about an hour.

When he had finished, speeches were made by Chiefs Black Moon, Sitting Bull, Two Bears, and Running Antelope. After about four hours, the Sioux decided to send a deputation to meet the commissioners.

The next morning, Father DeSmet and his party started back to Fort Rice, arriving June 30 to an enthusiastic greeting. The council between the Sioux and the U.S. commissioners took place two days later, and a peace treaty was signed by all the chiefs and principal warriors. Then, on July 3 and 4, presents were distributed and the council closed to the satisfaction of both parties.

Father DeSmet's achievement was one of the most remarkable in the history of the Indian wars. He was 68 years old and suffering from poor health, yet he journeyed 350 miles through rough and unknown country to parlay with a large force of Indians who had sworn death to all white men. By virtue of his great reputation among all the tribes, their absolute faith in his word, and their belief that he had their interests at heart, he succeeded in bringing peace, at least temporarily, to Indian country. The commissioners formally acknowledged that, without Father DeSmet, their work would have been a failure.

"We are all well aware," they wrote him, "that our thanks can be of little worth to you, and that you will find your true reward for your labors and for the dangers and privations which you have encountered, in the consciousness that you have done much to promote peace on earth and good will to men."

Father DeSmet stopped at Fort Sully on his way down the river, and finally arrived at St. Louis about August 30, 1868. A few months later, he sailed again for Europe, arriving at Termonde, his birthplace, in about the middle of December. In the spring, he visited the principal cities of Belgium, Holland, France, and England, and he sailed for America June 21. That fall, he visited Omaha, St. Mary's Mission in Kansas, and Chicago.

On June 1, 1870, Father DeSmet left St. Louis on his last voyage to Indian country. The purpose of this trip was to arrange for the establishment of a mission among the Sioux—an object which had long been dear to him but which he was never able to carry out. He returned to St. Louis early in August. Plagued by ill health, he remained there quietly, except for a brief visit to Chicago, until he left for Europe June 25, 1871. As on previous trips, he toured the principal cities from which he could elicit aid for the Indian missions. He left Europe April 1, 1872, and crossed the Atlantic for the last time. He remained in St. Louis for the rest of the year.

Ill health dogged Father DeSmet for much of his later years. In the winter of 1863–64, he was dangerously ill and expected to die. During his last trip to Europe, he experienced an almost fatal attack, and after his return to St. Louis in the spring of 1872, he did not again leave that city. The most serious of his physical ailments, and the one which finally proved fatal, was a form of Bright's disease, which afflicts the kidneys. Nevertheless, throughout 1872 he kept busy with the duties of his office and carried on a great deal of correspondence.

On May 13, 1873, Father DeSmet's most intimate personal friend, Captain Joseph LaBarge, was going to launch a new steamboat which he had named *DeSmet*. He asked the priest to bless the boat. Though ill, DeSmet did not want to decline his friend's request, particularly since the boat was named in his honor and was soon to visit the regions he knew and loved so well.

That evening, after the christening, his illness worsened severely. He underwent an operation, but it brought only temporary relief. On May 20, Father DeSmet asked to have the last sacraments administered to him, and he died on the morning of May 23, 1873.

Father DeSmet was buried in the little Cemetery of the Novitiate at Florissant, at the foot of the grave of a Father Verhaegen, who had come to America with him 50 years earlier. On the fifth anniversary of DeSmet's death, a 13-foot, six-inch bronze statue of him was unveiled in Termonde, his birthplace.

Father DeSmet was a man of great energy who fretted at sedentary work and was happiest when on the move. In the final 50 years of his life, he covered about 180,000 miles by the slow-moving conveyances of his day. He visited many parts of the United States, crossed the Atlantic 19 times, made one voyage around Cape Horn and two that involved crossing the Isthmus of Panama—all in the interest of his faith.

Father DeSmet's name is one of the most distinguished in the history of Catholic missionary work. He was a friend of the Indians to an extent never equaled by any other white man, and so there was never another white man for whom they felt the deep personal affection and absolute trust they did for him. He had but to show himself to win their hearts, and as years rolled past and they found him always true, their first impressions grew into a worshipful love.

4
William Jackson
Indian Scout for General Custer

Fate saved William Jackson, the adventurous grandson of Hugh Monroe, from slaughter at the Battle of the Little Bighorn. A scout for General George Armstrong Custer, he'd been ordered to ride with Major Marcus Reno on that infamous day in 1876. Jackson later worked as a guide and outfitter in the region that was to become Glacier National Park. *Courtesy of Gordon Pouliot*

Few works of fiction are as entertaining as the real-life adventures of Billy Jackson, a Montana frontiersman with Blackfeet blood in his veins. Yet, not many are familiar with the story of his exciting life or are aware that two outstanding scenic features of Glacier National Park bear his name—Mount Jackson and the Jackson Glacier.

His close friend, James Willard Schultz, wrote a fascinating book[3] about Jackson's first 21 years of life, with particular emphasis on his career as an army scout under the command of General George Armstrong Custer. But the story of his later years in the Northwest has yet to be told.

William Jackson was born at Fort Benton, Montana, on August 27, 1856, to Amelia and Thomas Jackson. His maternal grandfather was the legendary Hugh Monroe, who came west in 1815 to live with, and marry into, the Blackfeet tribe. His father's family was from Virginia.

Billy Jackson's early years were spent at Fort Benton, where his father worked as a tailor for the American Fur Company. He was surrounded by family—his parents; his only sibling, Robert, two years his senior; his grandfather, Hugh; his grandmother, Sinopah; two uncles, John and Frank, who assisted Hugh as post hunters; an unmarried aunt, Lizzie; and John's wife, Isabel. The entire family lived together in large and comfortable quarters within the company post.

In the mid-1800s, tiny Fort Benton was a place of great importance in the Northwest. Not only was it the only town in what was to become Montana, but it was headquarters for the fur trade in that part of the country. People called it the world's innermost port, since it was the head of navigation on the Missouri River, which flows more than 2,000 miles to St. Louis, Missouri, headquarters of the American Fur Company.

Most residents of Fort Benton were employed by the fur company. With few exceptions, they were Canadians or Mississippi River French Creoles, docile, hardworking men of happy disposition. They sang as they worked about the post, and in the evenings they played upon their fiddles and danced to old French songs their ancestors had brought across the seas in days long past. Conversation at the fort was in three languages: English, Creole French, and Pikuni, the latter Blackfeet tongue predominating. By the time Billy was six or seven years old, he was fluent in all three languages.

The men, women, and children of Fort Benton were like one big happy family that looked upon the company factor, Andrew Dawson, as a kindly father figure. It seemed as if the surrounding plains would always be black with buffalo, the Blackfeet would always have plenty of well-tanned robes and furs to trade, and the powerful steamboats of the great American Fur Company would come every spring from St. Louis with ample quantities of goods to trade. The youngsters expected eventually to take their fathers' places as bourgeois, clerks, traders, artisans, hunters, and laborers for the company at Fort Benton.

However, then came the winter of 1863–64 and with it, as Billy's grandfather often said, "rising black clouds of trouble and change."

Andrew Dawson, the factor at Fort Benton, decided to return to his native Scotland in hopes a medicinal spring there would cure lameness brought on by a fall he had suffered a few years earlier. All through the winter, Monroe had been talking about the mountains and his desire to camp again beside them. When Dawson left and a new factor was named, Monroe decided to go trap beaver in the mountains, and he insisted that his entire family go with him.

It took a week or more to prepare for the journey, since the family was taking all its property along. In addition to 20 or more packhorses and 10 saddle horses, there were about 70 free horses which were herded along at the rear of the column by the two Jackson boys and their Uncle Frank. At intervals along the line of loaded horses rode Uncle John, Thomas Jackson, and the four women.

Thomas Jackson had little enthusiasm for the outdoors. He had never cared to hunt and had never killed a buffalo or trapped a beaver. However, his sons idolized him because he was good to them, taught them to read and write, and had sent to St. Louis for toys, games, and storybooks for them. The previous Christmas, he had given each a new lightweight rifle, complete with well-filled powderhorn and ball-pouch, and boxes of caps. They looked forward to the trip as an opportunity to make use of their new guns.

After a day or two on the trail, the family made camp on the west bank of the outlet of beautiful Two Medicine Lake and opposite a red and gray mountain which they admired very much. Later, Billy Jackson and James Willard Schultz would name it Rising Wolf in honor of Hugh Monroe.) They constructed three lodges, all of them of new, well-tanned buffalo cow leather. One was occupied by John and his wife; the second by Hugh Monroe, his wife, Frank, and Lizzie; and the third by the Jackson family.

The next day, Hugh Monroe started up one of the valley trails, taking the two Jackson boys—and their rifles—with him. While Monroe's attention was elsewhere, the two boys stole away, hoping to get a shot at an elk or deer. At the lower end of a small grassy park, they saw the thick brush quivering. Thinking it was a buffalo, Robert fired, and out of the brush leaped a huge, angry grizzly. Clearing the brush, it stopped and sat up. Billy, although he wanted to turn and run, took careful aim and inflicted another wound. As the bear continued to bound toward them, Billy fled up the trail and leaped for the low branch of a cottonwood tree near the trail. As he did so, the bear struck at him, one of its claws ripping the lower part of his right trouser leg and cutting into the flesh.

As the bear was about to spring again at the boy, his grandfather's rifle gave a thunderous boom, and the bear suddenly sank quivering to the ground. Billy dropped to the ground and, too weak to stand, stared at the dying animal.

"What does this mean? What have you boys been doing?" cried their grandfather, hastily reloading as he stood over Billy, his blue eyes bright with anger.

Just then, brother Robert came running toward them, exclaiming: "Oh, what a whopper of a bear! We got him, didn't we?"

"Yes, and he all but got your brother! Let me hear all about it." After the boys told their story, Monroe exclaimed, "I've a good mind to give you a real switching! Both of you! Well, you've had a narrow escape, and let this be a lesson to you to never shoot at anything that you cannot see plainly. And another thing, you boys are not to go off by yourselves to hunt, and if you sneak away from me again when I take you out, I'll put your rifles where you can't get them again this summer!"

Monroe said the bear weighed about a thousand pounds. While skinning it, they found that Robert had shot it well back, Billy's bullet had pierced the end of one lung, and the fatal shot fired by Monroe had broken its neck. They brought the hide back to camp and dumped it on the ground in front of the lodges. Lizzie volunteered to flesh the hide, dry it, and tan it for a bed robe for the two boys.

In the next few days, they set their traps whenever they saw beaver dams, and while thus engaged they caught sight of a huge bull moose along the shallows of the lake shore. They made their way carefully through tangles of brush and high grass until they were within 50 yards of their prey. At Billy's request, his grandfather allowed him to take the first shot. The boy took careful aim and fired. The moose, mortally wounded, staggered toward the timber and collapsed after a few awkward leaps. They skinned it and took as much of its meat as they could carry.

When they returned the next day to find they had caught two or three beaver, they cautiously approached the remains of the moose and found an old mother grizzly and her cubs feeding on the carcass. Wary of the bears, they moved their traps up to the next lake, where they found plenty of beaver signs. On the first day at this new location, they caught 14 beaver and an otter. They continued to trap successfully, and on the sixth day they saw approaching 200 lodges of Kootenai Indians, led by their chief, Back-Coming-in-Sight.

The Kootenais were old friends of Hugh Monroe, and he welcomed them heartily. They had come across the Continental Divide to hunt and trap, and Monroe advised them to send messages to the Pikuni chiefs, seeking permission to hunt in Pikuni territory. He assured them their request would be granted.

The arrival of such a large party meant the end of trapping in that valley for the Monroe family, and so they collected their traps the next day and headed north.

On the second evening after they left the Two Medicine Valley, they arrived at the foot of Lower St. Mary Lake. They set up their lodges at the edge of a narrow grove of cottonwoods and built a corral for their horses well back in the timber. The next morning, they divided into two groups. Grandfather Monroe, Lizzie, and Billy set their traps along the little streamlets running down the big ridge into the lakes, while Robert, John, and Frank set out to trap down the river. Beaver were plentiful, and for several weeks their daily catch averaged 10 beaver. When it dropped off to three or four a day, they decided to move camp to the foot of the upper lake.

That evening, as they enjoyed a feast of moose meat, having finished packing their belongings, they heard their dogs mournfully baying in the darkness. Suddenly, several of the horses in the corral snorted, and the howling of the dogs changed to short, fierce barks. Suspecting either a grizzly or a hostile war party, the men seized their rifles and headed toward the corral, where a large war party of Assiniboines was trying to steal their horses.

The Monroes were greatly outnumbered, and their enemies not only succeeded in driving their horses out of the corral, but they returned to loot the lodges. Monroe had ordered the women to run through the timber and down to the ford of the river until the men were able to join them. The Assiniboines removed everything of value from the lodges, including their traps and beaver pelts, and then burned them to the ground.

When the family finally gathered at the campsite, Grandmother Sinopah sat down and wept bitterly. The Assiniboines had taken their traps, pelts, food, ammunition, and all but two of their horses. There was nothing left to do but give Amelia and Sinopah the mounts and head back to Fort Benton.

Near sundown of the following day, they reached the lower Two Medicine Lake, where they found that the Kootenai Indians had broken camp and gone down the river. They followed their trail the next morning, and late in the afternoon they discovered their camp at the mouth of Little Badger Creek.

The Kootenais were surprised to see them but extended a warm welcome and prepared a feast for the hungry Monroes. The menu included boiled buffalo boss ribs, pemmican, stewed *pommes blanches,* and, best of all, large servings of dried camas roots. Later, after Monroe had told of their misfortune, the Kootenais proved their friendship by outfitting the party with horses and saddles, pack animals, parfleches of dried meat, buffalo robes, a kettle or two, and a few cups. Three days later, camp was broken, and they all joined the Pikunis on the Bear River.

After many talks around their evening lodge fires, in which Tom Jackson would take no part, Hugh Monroe and his sons decided to go to Fort Benton and get on credit whatever traps, ammunition, and other gear were needed to cross the Missouri River and trap beaver along the streams flowing out of the Belt Mountains. They left the women in their former quarters at the trading post. The Jackson boys, having had a taste of wilderness, begged to join the men. Their father strongly objected, saying they were too young for such a dangerous life. However, when their grandfather said he would take them and when their mother interceded on their behalf, Jackson finally capitulated. Three days later, completely outfitted, the men and boys forded the river and struck off south across the plains for the Belt Mountains. Thomas Jackson was able to return to his former job as post tailor.

They trapped along the upper reaches of Deep Creek and the Judith and Musselshell Rivers, and in the latter part of November returned to Fort Benton with six packs of beaver skins, each weighing 90 pounds. They wintered at the fort and in the spring struck out again to trap, returning to Fort Benton late in the autumn with all the beaver packs their horses could carry.

So, trapping from early spring to late fall and wintering at Fort Benton, time passed all too quickly for the Jackson boys. Fort Benton was growing. Soldiers now occupied the old adobe fort, and one by one homes, stores, saloons, and a hotel were being erected. The one-time *engagés* of the American Fur Company resented the nearby discovery of gold that was bringing a horde of newcomers into the country.

In the spring of 1870, Grandfather Monroe decided to head north, away from civilization. Thomas Jackson declined to go along, saying he planned to take his family down the river to Fort Buford, where an old friend, Charles Larpenteur, was sure to give him a job. Robert was now 16 and Billy 14, and they argued for days to go with their grandfather. But in early April, their relatives packed and headed north without them.

After selling their horses, the Jacksons bought a small boat and loaded it with their few belongings. They set off down the Missouri, with Thomas steering and each of the boys working an oar. Aided by the four-mile-an-hour current, they made fast progress down the river. Generally, they cooked their suppers on islands, then drifted on in the dark to make fireless camps on other islands. They saw many animals.

Late one afternoon, they went ashore to shoot a deer they had seen. Suddenly, they were attacked by several Indians. The boys and their father started shooting and hit two of their attackers. In the meantime, the family had pushed the boat into the stream. A series of shots from the enemy missed them, one striking the boat. They landed on the opposite shore down-stream, and after that they did much of their traveling under cover of darkness, until landing at Fort Buford.

There they found Larpenteur crippled by a broken thigh. He needed an experienced clerk and gave Jackson the position. Within an hour, the family was comfortably quartered in a room of the post, two doors below the trade room. Larpenteur warned them that the Sioux and Yanktonnais encamped near the post were in an ugly mood. One evening they learned from a friendly Arikara-Sioux scout named Bloody Knife that the war party the Jacksons had encountered were Unkpapa Sioux. In their fight with the Jacksons, one of the Indians, Buffalo Rib, had been killed, and another, Red Star, had been wounded.

Bloody Knife and half a dozen full-blooded Arikaras served as army scouts and had quarters in the fort. The Jackson boys soon visited them and got acquainted. They began to learn the Arikara language and by summer's end were fairly fluent in it.

By August, plums and chokecherries had ripened in the breaks of the valley, and the boys' mother was eager to gather some. So the boys borrowed three saddle horses and set out with Amelia. As they rode, they saw many bands of horses, each guarded by a watchful Indian herder. In passing one of these bands, Robert recognized a big black and white pinto as one that had belonged to an uncle. Then he realized the entire band had recently been stolen from the Pikuni.

Robert wanted to retrieve the pinto at once, but then he noticed that the herder was one of the party that had attacked the family en route to Fort Buford. So they went on and had their sacks partially filled with plums when Robert, who had climbed to the top of the ridge, warned that enemies were coming—five of them. They mounted their borrowed horses and headed for the fort. As the enemies gained on them, they recognized the herder they had seen earlier. The boys made their mother ride on while they stopped and made ready to fire at the oncoming riders.

With carefully aimed shots, they brought down two horses, causing their pursuers to swerve into the brush and timber coulee. The Indians fired ineffectually, then remounted and tried to intercept the Jacksons on their route to the fort. However, the lay of the land favored the boys and their mother, and they were able to escape.

When they got back to the fort and told of their adventure, it created considerable excitement. The fort commander ordered the Arikara scouts and a company of mounted infantry to go in search of the hostiles, but they returned to the fort at midnight without having seen any of the enemy. When the boys saw Bloody Knife the next morning, he told them that Black Elk, Fox Eyes, and three other Sioux had recently arrived with a band of horses stolen from the Pikunis. They were the same Indians with whom the Jacksons had their fight while coming down the river. Bloody Knife warned them never to venture far from the fort for fear of being waylaid by Black Elk or other hostiles.

In September, impatient at being confined to the immediate vicinity of the fort, the Jackson boys began to frequent the quarters of the Arikara scouts. One of them gave the youths two good horses that a relative had left with him, and their father got them two condemned army saddles and bridles from the fort quartermaster. They began riding with the scouts as they went out on their rounds.

By December, the boys had decided to become army scouts. They went to see the fort commander and told him of their desire. Their request was denied because of their youth, but they were permitted to continue riding with the scouts. For quite some time, the scouts had little to do but hunt deer—rather tame sport for the Jackson boys, though better than being shut up in the post.

Another two years passed. In the spring of 1873, it was rumored that the line of the Northern Pacific Railroad was to be extended west from Bismarck, North Dakota, and that surveyors would soon be choosing a route across the plains to the Yellowstone River. Some thought it would mean settlement of that part of the country and the end of troubles with the Indians. But Bloody Knife said it meant the beginning of real war with the Sioux and the Cheyennes. It was reported, too, that the Seventh Cavalry, under General George Armstrong Custer, would be stationed at the new army post, Fort Abraham Lincoln, and would furnish an escort for the railroad builders.

Billy and Robert were now more eager than ever to enlist with the scouts. Robert was 19 and Billy 17, and though they were fairly tall, they were very slender. So they went to the commander with Bloody Knife. This time, their request to enlist was approved, provided they could obtain the consent of their parents. Their father was unwilling to give his approval, saying it was too dangerous. However, their mother sided with them, and that night they slept in the scouts' quarters. A new life had begun for them.

Within a few days the steamboat *Far West* arrived, bringing news that the scouts were to embark on the first downriver boat and go to Fort Lincoln, where they would join the military escort that was to start west with the railroad surveyors. The steamboat *Luella* came from Fort Benton and took them to Fort Lincoln, where they were ordered to report to nearby Fort Rice, from which the expedition was to start. There, they learned that the famed Seventh Cavalry under General Custer would form the main part of the escort.

Much had been heard of Custer's bravery, but when he arrived the scouts were surprised to see him dressed in a fringed buckskin coat and trousers, boots with red leather tops, and a wide-brimmed soft hat, instead of the regulation officer's uniform. He rode his spirited horse with grace and ease, and his curly yellow hair hung down almost to his shoulders. From that moment, the scouts worshipped him. They named him Long-Yellow-Hair Chief, which they soon abbreviated to Long Hair. Bloody Knife soon became, among the scouts, his principal adviser.

On June 20, 1873, the escort of 80 officers and almost 1,500 enlisted men and scouts left Fort Rice for the Yellowstone country. They overtook the surveying party east of Heart River. About three weeks after leaving the fort, they reached the edge of the badland slopes of the Yellowstone Valley, where they rendezvoused with the steamboat *Far West* at the mouth of Glendive Creek. They rested a few days and then were ferried across the Yellowstone River. By August 4, they were near the mouth of the Tongue River, where they repulsed a surprise attack by 300 Sioux warriors without the loss of a single man.

Four days later and some 60 miles farther up the valley, the scouts found the trail of a large camp of Sioux. General Custer, with the scouts and four squadrons of the Seventh Cavalry—450 men in all—made a forced march to try to overtake the Indians.

Custer's men had lost time in crossing the river, and presently
they were attacked by a thousand Indians. Custer ordered his
men to charge. Surprisingly, the enemy retreated, having caught
sight of the main body of the expedition coming up the valley.
Custer and his men pursued the enemy for seven or eight miles,
but the last of them recrossed the river to safety. After remaining
in the general area for a time, the railroad surveyors, accompanied by the Seventh Cavalry and some of the scouts, including
the Jackson brothers, struck out for Fort Lincoln. They arrived
there without further adventure September 22. The rest of the
expedition returned some time later.

At Fort Lincoln, Robert and Billy were pleasantly surprised
to find their mother waiting for them. They built a little cabin
next to the scouts' quarters, and she lived there all winter,
returning to Fort Buford on the first steamboat headed upriver
in the spring.

The winter passed quietly, and with the approach of spring
came word that the Seventh Cavalry was to go to the Black Hills
to select a site for a fort and to learn if it were true that prospec-
tors had found placer gold there. The expedition, including the
Jackson brothers, left Fort Lincoln July 1, 1874. It was made
up of 10 companies of the Seventh Cavalry; one of the 17th
Infantry; a few members of the United States Engineers under
Colonel William Ludlow; 61 Indian Scouts; Charley Reynolds,
a white scout; and a long train of supply wagons. Accompanying the expedition were two geologists, N. H. Winchell and
George Bird Grinnell.

As the group moved south, it began to see the signal fires
of hostile Sioux camps, but it was never able to get within fir-
ing range of them. When the party arrived in the hills, it found
broad and fertile meadows, plenty of water, slopes of heavy
timber, and placer gold in the old channels of the streams.
Custer and the geologists were said to be writing reports about

the richness of the country, which by treaty belonged to the Sioux, Cheyennes, and Arapahoes.

The expedition returned to Fort Lincoln about the end of August without encountering any hostile Indians. Again, the fall and winter were uneventful, except for one bit of excitement. That was the capture and escape of Chief Rain-in-the-Face, who had been boasting at the Standing Rock Agency that he had murdered two white men, John Honzinger and Augustus Baliran, the veterinarian and the sutler of the Yellowstone expedition of 1873. By order of General Custer, he was arrested and brought to Fort Lincoln. He admitted the murders to Custer and was held prisoner in the guardhouse awaiting trial.

Rain-in-the-Face had many visitors, including Captain Tom Custer and his interpreter, Billy Jackson. The chief warned Custer he would never be executed, and he did escape. He reportedly fled into Canada and then eventually joined Sitting Bull's camp in the Powder River country.

In 1874 and 1875, the survey for the Northern Pacific Railroad was practically at a standstill because of the determined opposition of the Sioux. The expedition to the Black Hills had further enraged them. Sitting Bull sent messengers to the Northern Cheyenne, Arapaho, Assiniboine, Yanktonnais, and other tribes of the Sioux to join his hostile Unkpapas in preserving the last of their buffalo country from the inroads of the whites. In autumn of 1875, the hostile tribes were notified that if they did not report to their agencies and remain there, the soldiers would make them do so. The Indians defied the order, and when news of this reached Fort Lincoln, the army scouts held a grand council in February 1876. Bloody Knife warned that the Indians' defiance meant a big fight in which many of the scouts and soldiers would be killed. With this gloomy prediction, Robert and Billy Jackson agreed.

It was from Charley Reynolds, the white scout, that the Jacksons and the Indian scouts learned that the government had a grand plan to capture the hostile tribes, deprive them of their weapons, and force them to return to their agencies. General George Crook, with about a thousand troops, was to advance upon them from Fort Fetterman on the Platte River. Colonel John Gibbon, at Fort Ellis in western Montana, was to come east on the Yellowstone River with about 600 men. General Custer would come west from Fort Lincoln, and the three armies would surround the Indians in a pincer movement and crush them. The success of the mission depended on timing, since none of the three forces alone could accomplish the purpose.

General Crook's command was first in the field, but on March 17 it was so badly beaten by Crazy Horse's Sioux that it had to return to Fort Fetterman to reorganize. Increased to about 1,500 men, it left for the north May 29. Colonel Gibbon, with his command, left Fort Ellis March 30. The Fort Lincoln contingent was scheduled to leave on the morning of May 17 under the command of General Alfred Terry. Besides the Seventh Cavalry under Custer, there were to be two companies of the 17th Infantry, one of the Sixth Infantry, and one of the 20th Infantry, with three Gatling guns and a long wagon train and pack train. The scouts, including the Jacksons, were attached to the Seventh Cavalry. They brought the total number of men under Terry to almost 1,500.

Terry's command struck the Powder River about 20 miles above its mouth and camped there several days. From this camp, Major Marcus Reno moved south with part of the Seventh Cavalry and some of the scouts, while the rest of the command moved up to the mouth of the Tongue River. They reached the Tongue June 19, the same day as the steamboat *Far West*. That evening, two of Reno's scouts came in with word that they had found the trail of many hostiles heading west from Rosebud Creek to the Bighorn River. On the morning of the 21st, the united command camped at the mouth of Rosebud Creek. Across the river was Gibbon's command, and the *Far West* ferried Terry and his staff across for a grand council of war.

Since Reno's Crow scouts believed that the camp of the hostiles on the Rosebud numbered, at most, no more than 800 or 900 able-bodied warriors, Terry planned the campaign accordingly. He ordered Custer to go up the Rosebud to the Indian trail reported by Reno, to follow it westward, and to be prepared to attack the camp June 26, when he would be supported by Gibbon's command. The latter would proceed to the mouth of the Bighorn River and march up it to get in touch with Custer's command.

Custer, with the Seventh Cavalry, his scouts, and a pack train carrying 15 days' rations and extra cartridges, left the mouth of the Rosebud about noon June 22. The Jackson brothers rode with an old friend, Frank Girard, who had once been captured by the Sioux and was familiar with their ways. On June 24, they struck the trail of the hostiles—a trail so wide that the scouts estimated it had been made by at least 1,500 lodges, and Bloody Knife thought there might even be more. Bloody Knife warned Custer this gathering of hostile tribes was too large to attack, but Custer would not believe him. Both Bloody Knife and Charley Reynolds were sure they would not survive the battle. The Jacksons heard their words and were chilled by them.

Lieutenant Charles Varnum, in charge of the scouts, split them into three parties, with the Jacksons and Reynolds to follow the lieutenant on the trail. They moved cautiously, listening for sounds and looking for the gleam of lodge fires. They traveled through the night of June 24 with no sight or sound of the enemy. At dawn, Varnum reported to Custer, while the men rested and had breakfast.

Convinced that he could not surprise the enemy, Custer ordered a quick advance. In the meantime, the troops met John Bruyer and his two Crow scouts. They were excited, and Bruyer said to Custer, "General, we have discovered the camp, down there on the Little Bighorn. It is a big one! Too big for you to tackle! Why, there are thousands and thousands of Sioux and Cheyennes down there." For a moment the general stared at him, and then he sternly replied, "I shall attack them! If you are afraid, Bruyer . . ."

Custer called his officers together and ordered the attack upon the camp. In the meantime, Bruyer described the enemy camp, which he said was three miles long and made up of hundreds and hundreds of lodges. North, south, and west of it were thousands of horses being closely herded. Custer made a final speech to his men, exhorting them to fight hard and make every shot count. Billy heard Bloody Knife say, as he looked up at the sun, "I shall not see you go down behind the mountains tonight." Billy was saddened by the belief that his own end was near.

Lieutenant Varnum ordered the Jacksons to go with Major Reno's column, and they were soon in the saddle and headed down a narrow valley toward the river. They crossed the river and turned straight down the valley for more than a mile. A grove of timber prevented them from seeing the Indian camp at first, but when they had passed the timber they saw a great camp and hordes of riders coming from it to attack. The Jacksons turned into the timber and spurred their horses into a dry channel of the river, overgrown with timber and brush. Leaving their horses, they climbed up the bank as the rush of the enemy, at least 500 well-mounted riders in all their war finery, came by them. The shots, the war cries, and the thunder of horses' hooves were deafening.

As the enemy charged the soldiers' center and then swerved, Robert Jackson, at Billy's side in the brush, exclaimed, "Look at the one on the big white horse! He's Black Elk!" They both fired at him and he pitched head first from his horse.

As the Indians were about to out-flank Custer's men, an officer ordered the scouts to their horses. They saw Bloody Knife, Reynolds, and Girard mount. Major Reno, hatless, waved his six-shooter and sped off, shouting something that Billy couldn't hear. The scouts swarmed after him, heading back the way they had come, intending to recross the river and get up on the bluffs where they could make a stand. By this time, hundreds more Indians had come from the camp and engaged in hand-to-hand combat. Just in front of the Jacksons, Bloody Knife and Reynolds went down, meeting the fate they had foretold.

Billy and Girard found themselves cut off by more Indians coming from the direction of their camp, so they wheeled to the left and plowed back into the timber, constantly under fire. They finally got into thick, high brush and were forced to dismount and tie their horses. They were joined by Lieutenant Camilius De Rudio and Thomas O'Neil, both horseless. The men hid for several hours, and then Billy and Girard retrieved the two horses and, after a great deal of difficulty, forded the river. After becoming separated and unexpectedly finding each other again, they followed a trail up the slope from the river. Wandering farther, they stumbled onto a number of men from Captain Frederick Benteen's company and Robert Jackson.

They learned that Major Reno's detachment had withstood repeated attacks on its position, with 67 killed and 57 wounded. All would have been lost had not Benteen and then Captain Thomas MacDougall joined Reno after he reached the top of the bluffs. In about an hour, De Rudio and O'Neil appeared and received a hearty welcome. On June 27, Terry and Gibbon arrived with their troops, bringing the horrifying news that they had found General Custer and all of his command—dead, stripped, and mutilated.

There on the bluffs they buried Reno's dead as best they could. Terry's men carried the wounded down to their camp. Girard and Billy Jackson found their horses where they had left them, and they helped to bury Charley Reynolds, Bloody Knife, and others. Then they went to Custer's part of the battlefield and found that of the 203 men in the command, Custer was the only one neither scalped nor mutilated. Later, rumor spread that Chief Rain-in-the-Face had killed Captain Tom Custer and cut out his heart.

In the meantime, word had been sent to Grant Marsh, captain of the *Far West*, to bring his boat as far up the Bighorn River as possible. The men started down from the battlefield very slowly, as the wounded had to be moved with great care. At daybreak, the wounded were put aboard the *Far West*, which had come 40 miles up the Bighorn, and the steamboat started for Fort Lincoln. The 700-mile trip was made in a record 55 hours. When the boat arrived, 28 women at the fort learned they were widows. Amelia Monroe had come down from Fort Buford to get news of Robert and Billy, and she later told her sons that the grief of Mrs. Custer and Mrs. Calhoun, Mrs. Custer's sister-in-law, was heartrending.

After caring for its wounded, the command camped at the mouth of the Tongue River for a much-needed rest; then it moved to the mouth of the Rosebud, where reinforcements joined it—six companies of the 22nd Infantry under Colonel Ellis and six companies of the Fifth Infantry under Colonel Nelson Miles. In the meantime, there was much criticism of Major Reno from those who thought he should have been able to rejoin Custer and save the day. The scouts, however, including the Jacksons, thought Custer himself was fully responsible for his defeat. He had been warned by three different scouts that the enemy far outnumbered his troops, but he spurned any advice and decided to attack the hostiles before the troops of Terry and Gibbon could arrive. Moreover, he had lost all chance of winning the fight by splitting his command into three columns and sending Reno and Benteen so far away they could be of no assistance. As the scouts summed it up, General Custer, rashly brave, lost the battle of the Bighorn through his own fault.

As Gettysburg was the highwater mark for the South in the Civil War, so the Little Bighorn was the highwater mark for the American Indians in the losing struggle against the whites. Sitting Bull had taken skillful advantage of Custer's tactical errors and his desire to be a hero. But once the Sioux and their allies had achieved this crushing victory over the temporarily undermanned but overconfident white forces, they never again regained the upper hand. Instead, they tried to retreat, a difficult maneuver encumbered as they were by their women, children, and belongings.

After the battle of the Little Bighorn, the commands of Terry and Crook camped for a time at the head of the Rosebud River. Between them, they numbered six or seven thousand men. Such a force, far from a base of supplies, was unable to pursue the hostiles, now split up into a number of bands that could move faster than the soldiers could follow.

Terry sent what was left of the Seventh Cavalry to Fort Lincoln, but he transferred its scouts, including the Jacksons, to the command of Miles. The latter was to mop up—to hunt and capture or defeat the scattered bands of Sioux, if possible, and to complete construction of a fort at the mouth of the Tongue River. The last steamboat of the season to arrive at the Glendive camp brought two companies of the Seventh Infantry to help with the construction of the new post.

Shortly after the Seventh Cavalry scouts reported to Miles, Robert Jackson was sent to Glendive camp to scout for Colonel

Ellis. A little later, Billy was told to select three of the Indian scouts and to report to Colonel Ellis until further orders. En route they encountered a group of 15 or 20 Sioux, and in the fight that followed one of the scouts was killed. Billy and the other two were finally able to join a wagon train escorted by 200 soldiers, including Ellis and Robert Jackson. A running battle was fought, with heavy losses incurred by the Indians. After a second day of fighting, the wagon train reached Custer Creek, where it was met by Miles and all but two companies of his Fifth Infantry.

A truce was arranged between Miles and the Sioux leader, who proved to be Sitting Bull. When the truce broke down, the soldiers fought their way right through the Indian camp, destroying much of their food, clothing, and cooking utensils. The Indians retreated after a hard fight. The next day, the troops learned that a small party of the hostiles had turned north. This party included Sitting Bull and Chiefs Gall and Pretty Bear, with about 40 lodges of their Unkpapas. However, Sitting Bull made a renewed effort to regroup his forces, which led to a difficult fight in which nearly 50 of the Indians were killed or wounded.

The soldiers were too exhausted to pursue further, and so they returned to the mouth of Tongue River, arriving there January 13, 1877. White Bull's Cheyennes and Crazy Horse's Sioux had been so severely punished that they sought peace. By the middle of April, the Cheyennes and Crazy Horse's band had complied with the terms of surrender, and Sitting Bull's band had fled to Canada.

Chief Lame Deer and his band still remained at large and defiant. To contend with them, Miles' contingent was reinforced by four companies of the Second Cavalry from Fort Ellis. On May 1, 1877, the scouts, including the Jackson brothers, left the Tongue River camp to locate Lame Deer's camp. Four days later, they reported they had found his trail.

Shortly thereafter, a part of Miles' troops marched south and, at dawn, approached Lame Deer's camp of 50 lodges. Miles sent part of his mounted force to stampede the Indians' herd of horses up the valley, and he ordered the rest of his men to attack the camp. The Jacksons were standing with Miles and his orderly when they saw four Sioux approaching with a white flag. One of them was Lame Deer himself. Since the Indians supposedly wanted a truce, Miles insisted that they lay down their rifles. Lame Deer complied, but his nephew, Bad Ankle, refused.

The truce broke down after a shot, fired at Miles, struck and killed his orderly. As Lame Deer and Bad Ankle were fleeing, Robert and Billy took careful aim and killed them both. After most of the hostiles had been driven across the Rosebud, the soldiers destroyed their camp, which was rich in dried meat, buffalo robes, and furs, as well as saddles, bridles, and other articles that had belonged to Custer's ill-fated Seventh Cavalry. Miles lost four men and had six wounded, while there were many casualties among the Sioux.

The next day, the soldiers turned back with 500 enemy horses to the Tongue River camp. So ended the war with the Sioux and Cheyennes.

With the Indian war over, Billy Jackson left the army and returned to the part of the Northwest where most of the Pikuni tribe of Blackfeet was spending the winter. This was in the open valley at Cow Creek, a small tributary of the Missouri, near the Bear Paw and Little Rocky Mountains. Joe Kipp had agreed to trade with the Indians there. His 18-year-old protégé, James Willard Schultz, was also spending the early winter of 1877–78 at Cow Creek.

Among those who had lodges in the camp were Hugh Monroe and his family. Billy joined them, and soon he became known as Siksikai-kwan (Blackfeet man) because of his close association with the people of his mother and grandmother. Now 21, Jackson struck up a friendship with Schultz, and both became friends with Apsi (Arrow), an Indian of about their age. Schultz has related how, after Apsi had put strychnine in the carcass of a bull buffalo, the three of them returned days later to find the bodies of 11 gray wolves, several coyotes, and a golden eagle.

One day, as the trio was about to visit another of Apsi's baits, a herd of buffalo thundered by, and the young men glimpsed in the middle of the herd a very rare sight—a white buffalo. Apsi followed the herd, hoping to shoot the sacred animal. Jackson and Schultz shot a fat buffalo cow and returned to camp with the meat.

The next morning, Apsi was again joined by Schultz and Jackson, and they followed the herd until Apsi was able to dispatch the white buffalo with a single shot. The three returned to camp with the white cow's hide and presented it to Red Eagle, the tribal medicine man, who accepted it and uttered a fervent prayer to the sun, asking for mercy and beneficence.

Hugh Monroe, a good Catholic, celebrated Christmas that year with a special feast at his spacious lodge for all his family, including grandson Jackson. Among the others invited were Joe Kipp, Schultz, and Red Eagle. After the meal was over, Monroe, at the request of Red Eagle, entertained the guests with a story of the hunt for the black antelope, an animal as rare as the albino buffalo, and considered sacred.

During the 1880s, Schultz established a business as a guide and outfitter. In 1891, he invited Billy to help him lead the notable party of George Bird Grinnell, Henry L. Stimson, and William H. Seward III on a month-long trip through the region that was to become Glacier National Park. They explored the Upper St. Mary Lake region and the Blackfeet glacier. It is the shrunken part of that ice field that is now the Jackson Glacier visible from the Going-to-the-Sun Road. On this trip, Grinnell named Mount Jackson and discovered that he and Jackson had both been with Custer on his 1874 expedition to the Black Hills.

Stimson many years later published a book entitled *My Vacations* in which he described his first visit to the St. Mary area. He had the following to say about Billy Jackson:

One of these (Jackson and Schultz) was a famous character. He was a quarter-breed Blackfoot Indian known as Billy Jackson who had served as one of Custer's scouts in the battle of the Little Bighorn far away to the south of us, and his tale of how he escaped from that disaster was a thriller when told over our campfire.

In the early 1890s, Jackson acquired a ranch in the Cut Bank Valley, although he continued to take occasional temporary assignments elsewhere. During the autumn of 1893, he spent a month as guide for Dr. Walter B. James and a Dr. Draper, of New York. Most of their time was spent hunting in the Cut Bank Valley, where game was plentiful. While there, Dr. James made a second effort to climb Flinsch Peak, south of Cut Bank Pass, since he had been unable to reach its summit the previous year.

Later that fall, Jackson headed a posse of Indian police and others in an effort to capture a gang which, in holding up and robbing a Great Northern train, had killed one man and wounded another. They pursued the robbers over the mountains, exchanging shots. The fleeing robbers were headed off by a group from Kalispell, which killed two of them and captured the other two.

In 1896, Jackson served as guide and packer for a federal commission that had been appointed by President Grover

Cleveland to help formulate a national policy for the U.S. Forest Reserves. The commission was composed of Gifford Pinchot, later governor of Pennsylvania, and Henry S. Graves, later chief forester and dean of the School of Forestry at Yale University.

Walter McClintock, just out of Yale, was employed as a photographer, and Billy Jackson and Jack Monroe, a white man who married into the Blackfeet tribe, were employed as guides. The survey was to be conducted on the west side of what is now Glacier National Park.

When the survey was completed, Jackson invited young McClintock to visit him at his ranch, and they traveled eastward across the Rockies by way of Cut Bank Pass.

At his ranch, Jackson raised hay, horses, and cattle. Then about 40 years old, he had an attractive young wife named White Antelope and four small children. Their home was a cabin of two rooms built of pine logs with sod-covered roof and clay-chinked walls; they also had corrals, low-lying sheds, and a garden.

In his book, *Old Indian Trails*, published in 1923 by The Riverside Press, McClintock described Jackson as having the swarthy complexion, black hair, and high cheekbones of an Indian. He was tall and slender, with an impressive manner, fluent of speech, polite and suave. He was liked and respected by both whites and Indians. Honest and industrious, generous and kind, he was always ready to help any who came to his ranch.

According to McClintock, Jackson was a good scout in the wilderness. He knew the trails and mountains and handled with skill the wild Indian horses. Self-reliant in time of danger, he was manly and courageous. He had a keen sense of humor and a wonderful knowledge of nature—information not gained from books. He knew woodcraft, as well as Indian legends, traditions and stories of war and adventure. In addition to fluent English, he spoke the Blackfeet and Cree languages.

Jackson took McClintock to the nearby camp of the Black-feet and introduced him to the head chief, White Calf, and his wife, Catches-Two-Horses, as well as many other Blackfeet notables. The Indians liked McClintock, and Chief Mad Wolf made him his adopted son.

In 1902, when writer Emerson Hough came at the sugges-tion of George Bird Grinnell to visit the future Glacier Park, he made arrangements with Schultz to act as guide. Schultz, in turn, engaged the services of Billy Jackson to be the third man on the trip. The expedition was unusual in that it was being undertaken in winter (February), and it was headed into the mountains near Nyack Creek and Loneman Mountain. With special gear furnished by Hough, the trio spent an uncomfort-able 10 days, hunting despite subzero temperatures and snow that reached a depth of 10 feet. When Hough chose to return to the eastern part of the mountains in September, Jackson was engaged to serve as guide on a hunting trip for Henry Stimson and Gifford Pinchot.

Later that year, Billy Jackson died suddenly as a result of illness.

5

Joseph Kipp

Trader with the Indians[4]

Prospector, army scout, trader, rancher—Joseph Kipp's many enterprises made him a familiar face among the Blackfeet Indians who dominated northern Montana and southern Alberta in the mid- to late 1800s. *Courtesy of Glacier National Park Archives*

Joseph Kipp was born in 1847 at Fort Union, the American Fur Company post at the mouth of the Yellowstone River. His mother was Sah-kwi-ah-ki (Earth Woman) and his father was James Kipp, then in charge of trade at Fort Union. His parents were unusual people.

James Kipp was born in Montreal, Quebec, in 1798 to a noted family of French *émigrés*. He came to the United States in the early 1820s, and in 1828 he entered the service of the American Fur Company. His ability, courage, and trustworthiness were soon recognized by the heads of the company, and he became its mainstay in the upper Missouri country. In 1832, artist George Catlin found him in charge of the company's post at the village of the Mandans, near present-day Bismarck, North Dakota. Prince Maximilian von Wied was his guest the following year and spoke very highly of him in his *Travels*.

When the company decided to build a post farther up the Missouri River, James Kipp was the only employee who would undertake such a dangerous assignment. He left Fort Union early in the spring of 1831, and that summer he built Fort Piegan at the mouth of the Marias River. When the post was burned by wandering Indians, he returned to Fort Union, resuming his job as factor. In 1860, Kipp retired from the fur trade and returned to Missouri to spend the rest of his life with his white family on a farm. He died in St. Charles, Missouri, in the summer of 1881, at the age of 83.

Joe Kipp's mother was born about 1815, and she married James Kipp in about 1832. She was the daughter of the great Mandan chief, Mah-to-to-pah (Four Bears), of whom Catlin wrote, "He is one of the finest and most courteous gentlemen that I ever met."

Among the Pikunis she was known as Earth Woman, and, according to James Willard Schultz, she was a woman of noble character and kindly disposition. She was like a second mother to Schultz, and she was a friend to all the poor and afflicted, white and red, as was her inseparable companion, an Arikara named Crow Woman.

Since Joe Kipp spent most of his youth at Fort Union and at the newer company post in Fort Benton, he became acquainted with the various Indian tribes of the area—Pikuni, Sioux, Gros Ventre, Crow, Mandan, and Arikara—and he learned to speak the language of each. In the early 1860s, an incident occurred at Fort Union that offers insight into Kipp's character.

The Crows had surprised a wandering family of Pikunis and killed all but a boy about Kipp's age, whom they kept as a slave. He met Kipp when the Crows came to Fort Union to trade, and he cried as he told of the loss of his parents, of his suffering, and of his longing to return to his own people. Kipp went at once to his father and persuaded him to buy the boy from his captors.

Shortly thereafter, the young Pikuni was stricken with smallpox, then endemic in the country. Young Kipp took the boy into his own room and nursed him to health, then sent him to Fort Benton and his own people on the first boat traveling upriver that season. The boy became a leader among the Pikunis, a great warrior and wise counselor in affairs of the tribe. He was Tail-Feathers-Coming-Over-the-Hill, and he eventually outlived his benefactor.

During James Kipp's long absences from the upper Missouri country, he left his son and wife in the care of various factors of the American Fur Company, particularly Andrew Dawson, who was in charge of the post at Fort Benton. In 1864, when the Company sold the post to George Steel and Matthew Carroll, young Kipp entered their employ and began a life of adventure.

At that time, Steel had a black horse renowned as the swiftest and best-trained buffalo runner in the country.[5] One of young Kipp's duties was to take care of the animal, which was kept in a stable at the rear of the fort. One morning, Kipp found the padlock of the stable door broken, the corral gate open, and the black horse missing. The Pikunis had long coveted it, so he guessed that the horse was in their big camp, which traders and fort employees were forbidden to enter.

Young Kipp felt so bad about the loss of the horse that he became physically sick. He begged to be allowed to try to recover it, but he was told not to take such a risk. In the meantime, old Four Bears, camp crier for the Pikuni chiefs, came into the fort and boasted long and loudly about White Antelope's "big, powerful, swift black horse." His boasting drove young Kipp almost mad, and one night, regardless of the consequences, he stole out of the fort and over the hill to the Pikuni camp. With a blanket wrapped about him, Indian fashion, and with a six-shooter in his hand, he wandered about among the lodges until he found White Antelope's tipi. White Antelope was giving a feast inside, and young Kipp, who understood Pikuni, heard him tell his guests how he had stolen the wonderful black buffalo runner.

Although the night was very dark, Kipp found the horse picketed near the lodge, cut its tie rope, and, using the short end for a bridle, mounted, thundered through the camp, and headed for the fort. Indians rushed madly from their lodges, and several fired at him. A dozen or more men mounted and gave pursuit, but none could stop him. The boy rode triumphantly into the fort.

Now it was Kipp's turn to boast. Whenever old Four Bears came into the trade room, the boy would cry out in imitation of a warrior counting his coups the details of how he had stolen into the Pikuni camp and ridden the black horse back to the fort. Old Four Bears was offended, and one day when Kipp had ended his singsong boast, the Indian hissed that White Antelope had threatened to kill Kipp the first time they met outside the fort.

The meeting soon came. Kipp went out hunting with Baptiste Rondin, the post hunter, and, topping a hill, he saw White Antelope coming on the trail. Rondin had already turned back with the men driving the meat carts, and, stubbornly, the boy did not call for help. He rode on, rifle cocked and ready but with a terrible fear in his heart. As they grew closer, warrior and boy glared grimly at each other, then met and passed. Young Kipp would not turn in his saddle to look back. So ended his second experience with real danger. Later, White Antelope became his friend. For recovering the horse, Steel rewarded Kipp with a year's schooling in St. Joseph, Missouri.

In 1868, Kipp, Charles Thomas, and John Wrenn went prospecting along the foot of the Rockies as far north as Edmonton, Alberta. They were probably the first gold seekers to examine that long stretch of country, and they found no gold. On their way north, they inadvertently left a pair of pincers at a camp on a small stream not far north of the Canadian border, and they did not miss it for several days. When they needed to shoe a bull, they discovered their loss, and Kipp went back for it. He named the stream along which it had been left Pincer Creek, the name it bears today.

The prospecting party was not well received at Fort Edmonton. The men encamped at the Hudson's Bay Company post had no love for the "Long Knives," as they called the men of the United States, because the American Fur Company had taken from the Hudson's Bay Company much of the trade with the Blackfeet tribes. But winter had set in, and Thomas and Wrenn elected to remain at the inhospitable post until spring rather than risk traveling through deep snow in extreme cold.

Kipp, however, was so homesick that he chose not to stay. On Christmas Day, he struck out southward with a young French Canadian, each riding a good horse and carrying a buffalo robe and a couple of blankets for bedding. They took no food, expecting to kill all the meat they wanted, but they found that buffalo and other big game had largely deserted the plains country. They did manage to kill a rabbit the first or second day, but for some days thereafter they were entirely without food.

One evening when they were hungry and weak, they uncovered a mouse nest and managed to kill three of the rodents. Instead of eating them, Kipp built a decoy fire, split open the mice and sprinkled them with strychnine, laid them near the fire, and went to sleep by another fIre a distance away. In the morning, he and his companion found a frozen wolf that had been poisoned by the bait. The wolf meat lasted until they reached the Belly River, where they killed a fat buffalo cow, made camp upon an island, and had a real feast.

From there to Fort Benton, the plains were black with buffalo, and they fared well. The last day of the long, hard trip was an eventful one. At the Goose Bill River, and again when approaching the Teton, they were chased by hunters from a Kainah, or Blood, camp. Both times they were nearly caught by the hostiles.

In 1869, Kipp became an army scout. He was stationed at Fort Shaw when his superior, Major Eugene Baker, was ordered to find and wipe out Black Weasel and the warriors of his band of the Pikuni in retaliation for the murder of Malcolm Clarke at his ranch near Helena. The command struck the trail of Heavy Runner's friendly band instead, and Kipp explained in vain that it was the wrong band. All Indians were alike to Baker, and he ordered Kipp to lead on, assigning two soldiers to keep at his back and shoot him if he made a false move.

So it was that, at daybreak on January 23, 1870, the soldiers looked down at the lodges of the friendly camp from the bank of the Marias River. Again Kipp pleaded with Baker not to molest the band. Again, his pleading was in vain, and Baker ordered his men to shoot and spare none. A dreadful carnage ensued. Men, women, children, and babes in arms were indiscriminately killed. Only three or four of Heavy Runner's men escaped. Later, Kipp had a hard time convincing the Pikunis that he had tried his best to save their kin, but they finally believed him.

After the Baker massacre at the Marias, Kipp resigned his position as an army scout and, forming a partnership with Charles Thomas, became a trader with the Indians, as his father had been before him. That spring, a new U.S. marshal was appointed, with headquarters at Helena, and his first official act was to proclaim his intent to enforce rigorously the laws relating to the introduction and possession of liquor in Indian country. This was a terrible blow to Fort Benton, which was located in Indian country.

At that time, Fort Benton was the only settlement of any importance on the upper Missouri River. Though it was small, it was headquarters for that part of the country, and it was the center of the great fur trade of the Northwest. The steamboats that came every spring from St. Louis with goods for the traders and supplies for Helena and other mountain camps went back with tremendous tarpaulin-covered bales of buffalo robes and pelts of beaver, wolf, deer, elk, and antelope.

Until the new marshal, whose name was Harding, slipped into Fort Benton and confiscated several cases of liquor, the traders could not believe he really meant to interfere with their business. Then they realized that their liquor trade would disappear unless they could devise some way to outwit him. The Blackfeet, the Gros Ventre, and other tribes demanded liquor along with trade articles of luxury and necessity, and the Indians threatened to transfer their trade to the Hudson's Bay Company posts to the north if the Long Knives could not supply it.

Kipp sought out his old friend and prospecting partner, Charles Thomas, and proposed that they cross the international boundary and build a post in Canada. He revealed a plan for getting the contraband goods across the line, and Thomas finally agreed to join the scheme. While Harding was in Fort

Benton, Kipp slipped away to Helena and bought 75 cases (750 gallons) of high-proof alcohol from Murphy, Neil & Co., to be delivered to the fork of the Missouri just below town.

Harding appeared and watched Kipp's every move, but then he went back to Fort Benton to keep an eye on things there. As soon as Harding left Fort Benton, Kipp had the alcohol taken to the river and loaded onto rafts. Then he set forth downstream with his awkward craft, heading for the mouth of the Sun River, a trip that he accomplished with great difficulty. At Sun River, he found Thomas waiting for him with three four-horse teams and wagons, some teamsters, and a man named Scott who had agreed to act as cook. The liquor was soon loaded onto the wagons, and within an hour the party started north by way of the Indian and Red River cart trail, later known as the Sun River Trail.

Three days later, just after crossing the north fork of the Milk River, the outfit saw a lone horseman approaching. Realizing it must be the marshal, Kipp said, "We may as well stop right here and stand him off."

The marshal passed the first and second wagons and rode on to the third, which Kipp was driving at the time.

"Well, Joe, I've got you at last," he said. "Just turn around and head for Fort Benton."

"Harding, you are just twenty minutes too late," Kipp answered. "You should have overtaken us on the far side of the creek back there."

"Oh, come. No joshing. This is serious business. Turn your team," the marshal insisted.

"Harding, right here you are no more a marshal of the United States than I am, for right here we are in Canada; the north fork of Milk River is the line," Kipp said.

Harding almost fell from his horse in surprise, and it was several minutes before he spoke. The international boundary line had not yet been surveyed and marked. No one knew where the monuments would eventually stand, but it was generally believed that Chief Mountain and the north fork of the Milk River were upon, or very close to, the 49th parallel.

After some quick thinking, Harding replied, "You have no proof that we are in Canada. I'll take chances that we are south of the line. I arrest you all for having liquor in your possession in the Indian country. Come, turn your outfit and we will strike out for Fort Benton."

Kipp laughed. "Marshal," he said, "you have no proof that we are not north of the line. Anyhow, we take the chance that we are in Canada and we are five against you—five to one. Right here we stand you off."

Harding argued and threatened, but his words were wasted. Suddenly he wheeled his horse around and, without even a wave, galloped away. Later, surveyors revealed that the spot where he had tried to make the arrest was about 300 yards south of the border.

Kipp and his outfit continued north to the Belly River and there built a trading post. They named it Fort Standoff to commemorate their interview with the marshal. While the place was being built, the teams were kept busy hauling trade goods and provisions from Fort Benton. With the coming of winter, the Blackfeet—Kainahs and Pikunis—gathered on the Belly and Old Man's Rivers according to an agreement with Kipp. The country was black with buffalo, and the Indians were industrious; by spring, the warehouse held nearly 3,000 fine robes and more than 2,000 small skins, mainly antelope and wolf. The trade room was bare of goods.

As will be noted later, Kipp's invasion of the Hudson's Bay Company territory had unforeseen and surprising results. The building of Fort Standoff proved to be of momentous consequence to the Canadians.

The arrival of the Fort Standoff robes in Fort Benton was the cause of as much excitement as a new discovery in a mining camp. The season there had been a fallow one. Under the watchful eye of Marshal Harding, traders had been unable to make a move, and they lost no time in preparing to invade the north country as Kipp had so successfully done. The leader of the rush was John H. Healy, one of the bravest and most picturesque characters of the Northwest. He was later sheriff of Chouteau County and still later the leading trader of Dawson City, Alaska, where he made and lost a fortune of more than a million dollars.

Kipp eventually learned that the factor of Fort Calgary had sworn vengeance against the American invaders of his territory and had vowed to clean out Fort Standoff. Not many years earlier, the Hudson's Bay Company factor at Fort Edmonton, Richard Hardesty, had incited the North Blackfeet to capture and destroy Fort Benton, and the company might have succeeded if the Pikuni women living there hadn't learned of the plan and shared it with their white husbands.

Bearing this in mind, Healy formed a partnership with A. B. Hamilton, and together they built a post at the junction of the St. Mary and Belly Rivers that was large and strong enough to withstand any assault by the Hudson's Bay Company. The place was built on the plan of Fort Benton, and real cannon were mounted in the bastions, with plenty of "grape and canister" beside them in the shape of 25-pound sacks of trade balls. The post cost $20,000 to build, and, most appropriately, it was named Fort Whoop-Up, in accordance with the owners' intention of "whooping-up" things in the north country.

In the meantime, Kipp and Thomas purchased a bull train with part of their winter profits and, abandoning Fort Standoff, built Fort Kipp at the junction of the Belly and Old Man's Rivers. It was not a pretentious place. Some rough log cabins were put up to form three sides of a square, and there was no stockade across the fourth, or south, side facing the rivers. Unlike Healy and Hamilton, they believed a fortified post was unnecessary.

The only noteworthy thing that took place the following winter at Fort Kipp was the killing of Calf Shirt, chief of the Kainahs. He was a man of vicious temper who had killed many of his own people just for the fun of seeing them drop. The whole tribe was glad to hear of his end.

During the summer and fall, great quantities of legitimate trade goods were hauled by bull train to the two forts from Fort Benton, and plenty of alcohol was brought out by fast four-horse teams, despite the watchfulness of the marshal. The Blackfeet, Sarcees, and Gros Ventres brought in many robes and wolf and antelope skins. Trade was good, with Kipp getting as much of it as his rivals at the more pretentious post. The success of the two firms was so marked that during the ensuing summer other Bentonites came north to get a share of the trade, notably J. D. Weatherwax, who built a post just below Fort Kipp. The following winter, 1873–74, all the posts did a fine trade, with something like 9,000 robes going to Fort Benton the following spring.

In the meantime, the Hudson's Bay Company had urged the Dominion Government to come to its aid and suppress the American traders. In the summer of 1874, a large detachment of North West Mounted Police was sent west from Winnipeg. Luckily for the traders, an Indian saw the Mounties approaching and gave the alarm in time for the Americans to cache their contraband goods. Weatherwax, however, refused to believe the news, and the police, finding liquor on his premises, confiscated his whole outfit.

So ended the contraband trade in the North. Unwittingly, Joseph Kipp had caused the westward movement of the North West Mounted Police. The all-powerful fur company that had urged their coming had lost its monopoly in western Canada.

The police revealed to the world the riches of the country, and soon railroads were built into it and the plains were over-run with settlers. In 1878, the last of the buffalo herds on the Saskatchewan plains migrated south of the border, never to return.

Luckily for Kipp and Thomas, the Mounties arrived before the pair had stocked up for the winter trade. The traders abandoned Fort Kipp and returned to Montana, where they began ranching near the present site of Dupuyer. They raised cattle for several years and freighted goods with their bull train between Fort Benton and the mountain towns. In 1877, they sold the ranch to James Grant and dissolved their partnership. Kipp returned to the trading business, following the Pikunis to their winter location and setting up a temporary post nearby. That winter, James Willard Schultz joined his staff.

Buffalo were not plentiful in the Marias country that winter, and trade was light. A few small herds tarried awhile in the vicinity of the Sweetgrass Hills to be chased about by the Pikunis, and the survivors drifted eastward toward the Bear Paw Mountains and southward across the Missouri River, where great numbers of their kind still roamed.

Late in the following summer, the Pikuni chiefs met with Kipp and proposed to hunt in the Bear Paw–Missouri River country if he would trade with them. He agreed to do so and went with them in October, after loading his bull team with goods at Fort Benton. The winter was spent along the southern slopes of the Bear Paws and at the head of Crow Creek. Game was plentiful. The Indians tanned a great many robes, but Kipp did not get half of them because his bulls were ailing and unable to make more trips for goods. In the spring, he took into Fort Benton 1,500 robes and about that number of small skins.

The following summer, 1879, the Pikunis proposed to winter in the Judith country if Kipp would trade with them there.

Again he agreed to do so and went on ahead of them to build a substantial log post on the Judith at its junction with Warm Spring Creek. Game was apparently as plentiful there as it ever had been. Elk roamed the mountain slopes in great herds; deer hid in every thicket and draw. Antelope swarmed on the plains, and buffalo grazed everywhere up to the edge of the pines. There was only one settler in the whole country, "Governor" Brooks, who was running a bunch of cattle on Warm Spring Creek and having trouble keeping them from running off with the buffalo.

The Pikunis arrived before winter, and with them came part of the Kainah tribe from the north. Kipp began trading with them for prime robes. Small skins came over the counter in a steady stream from sunrise to sunset everyday. A group of white hunters camped near the Kipp camp, each man killing 10 to 30 elk and deer a day.

Kipp handled no liquor that winter. Farther up the Judith River, a man named Juneau was trading whiskey to a small band of Red River half-bloods. Early in the winter, some of the Pikunis went to trade a few robes for liquor and got into a row with the Red River hunters which ended with the shooting of two of them. After that, the Pikunis kept away from Juneau's camp, much to the satisfaction of Kipp and Schultz.

Two anxiety-provoking incidents occurred that winter. The first involved John Healy, sheriff of Chouteau County, who came out to arrest a Kainah Indian named Turtle for the murder of Charles Walmsley on Cut Bank Creek some months earlier. The Kainahs swore they would not allow Healy to take Turtle, and the Pikunis were inclined to side with the Kainahs. Healy slipped handcuffs on the Indian, led him into the post, and chained him to a big, log roof support. A crowd of Kainahs and some young Pikunis surged in after him, and trouble appeared imminent, for Healy was obdurate and would not release his man.

It was Kipp who saved the day, and he had a strenuous time of it. He argued and pleaded more than two hours before he finally persuaded the Indians to allow Healy to take his prisoner to Fort Benton. Even after the last of the Indians filed out of the room, Kipp and Schultz could not be sure they would keep their word, and the post crew sat up all night. The crucial moment would come the next morning, when Healy would put Turtle into the buggy for the trip to Fort Benton.

Shortly before daylight, Kipp went out into the camp, aroused White Calf, Little Dog, and Running Crane, chiefs of the Pikunis, and asked them to go among the Kainahs and advise them against trying to take Turtle from the sheriff. They did as requested, but by the time Healy had led Turtle out of the post and chained him to the buggy seat, a big and surly crowd had gathered.

Had Turtle resisted or cried out for help, the whites would certainly have been killed. But the prisoner went peaceably because he thought there was no proof he had committed the crime. As a matter of fact, one of his companions had confessed to the killing. Turtle was found guilty and sentenced to pass the remainder of his life in the Detroit penitentiary.

The second anxious moment took place in early March, when a Lieutenant Crouse arrived at the post with a company of mounted infantry from Fort Benton. He informed Kipp that the War Department had ordered the Pikunis to return to their reservation. Settlers in the Judith country had complained that the Indians were killing their cattle, he said. According to Schultz, the message was the most unpleasant Kipp ever translated as an interpreter. The Pikunis had killed no cattle, White Calf said. Why should his people eat distasteful meat, he asked, when they had their choice of fat, good meat—antelope, buffalo, elk, and deer?

Crouse said he did not doubt that the Great Father had been misinformed, but orders were orders and he must escort the tribe back to its agency. For a time it looked as though war was about to break out. The young warriors, almost to a man, proposed to resist the soldiers, regardless of consequences. They would not listen to their chiefs, who were unwillingly counseling submission to the officer's demand. It was Kipp who finally brought them to their senses.

"Remember what the soldiers did to your people on the Marias," he told them. "If you don't want to lose the rest of your women, your children and little babies, then pull down your lodges and start north."

At last, one of the Indians cried, "'Enough! You have said enough. For ourselves we do not care, but we do care for our women and little ones. Because of them we will do what the young soldier chief says must be done."

And so, in direct violation of their treaty rights, the Pikunis were forced from a rich hunting ground to their reservation, absolutely bare of game. Their horses were poor, the new grass had not yet come up, and hundreds of the animals dropped along the trail. Kipp had the bull train loaded with the winter's trade, 1,800 robes and 3,000 small skins, and he journeyed with the Pikunis to Fort Benton.

By this time, practically all the buffalo left in Montana—or in the United States for that matter—were grazing within the great triangle of plains and mountains between the Missouri and Yellowstone Rivers. After a careful reconnaissance of the country, Kipp decided that Carroll, on the south bank of the Missouri, 30 miles above the mouth of the Musselshell River, would be the best location for trade—provided he could convince the Indians to hunt there for the winter. The Siksikas, Kainahs, and Crees of Alberta agreed, and Kipp, Schultz, and Eli Guardipee headed for Carroll early in July 1880 on the steamboat *Red Cloud.* On board with them was a large stock of goods, and more was sent overland by bull train.

At Carroll, the traders built a large warehouse, store, and cookhouse. The Indians arrived before the buildings were finished, and trade for small skins began at once. Buffalo were numerous, and as soon as their winter coats had thickened, trading in them began, too. When spring arrived, Kipp counted 4,000 prime robes which were sold to John Guwey of Boston. I. G. Baker & Co. of Fort Benton bought the small skins, principally antelope and deer.

Early in the summer of 1881, Louis Riel, leader of the Red River half-bloods, arrived at Carroll and made it his headquarters for the next year. It was there that he planned the invasion of Canada that would lead to his death. Kipp tried to reason with him, pointing out that he would have the whole English nation to fight, but Riel would not listen. Because Kipp would not help him with his plans, Riel suddenly transferred his trade to a nearby post. He never paid the bill of $700 he owed to Kipp.

That summer, Kipp did a good trade in small skins, dried meat, and pemmican. The food was sold in the north and east, eventually reaching the Sioux agencies. Although the days of the buffalo were obviously numbered, Kipp did a good business in the winter of 1881–82. Twenty-three hundred head and tail robes were taken in, along with about the same number of small skins. By the following winter, however, only a few small bands of buffalo remained, and their only hunters were a few English and Scottish half-bloods. The Siksikas, Kainahs, Crees, and Riel's French Crees had hunted their last buffalo and gone north. When spring came, the big warehouse was a melancholy sight: In one corner was a little pile of 300 hundred robes; in another were 400 antelope and deer skins.

So ended the fur trade on the Montana plains. After Kipp and Schultz had inspected the meager result of the winter's trade, Kipp prepared to abandon Carroll. "I was born in the buffalo trade," he said. "I expected to die in it. The buffaloes are gone; I don't know what to do."

Dismal as the outlook seemed, there was a silver lining. Kipp could reunite with his family. He had not been able to take his wife and children on winter trading expeditions, not only because of the danger and hardships involved, but also because of the logistical problems of housing and feeding them.

Kipp had married Double Strike Woman in 1877. She was a daughter of Chief Heavy Runner, who was killed in the Baker Massacre. Their children were Mary, James, and George. The Kipps also adopted the children of Double Strike Woman's dead sister—William and Margaret Fitzgerald. Kipp was devoted to all his children, giving them every advantage possible, including an education in Spokane, Washington.

With no training or experience other than trading, Kipp began to turn his hand to whatever seemed available. He left the store and post office at Carroll for Schultz to manage and built a sawmill at the fort. He hauled lumber by bull team to Fort Benton. With partners, he built at Robare the first irrigation ditch in Montana, selling it later to the Conrad Investment Company (now the Pondera County Canal and Reservoir Company).

At the same time, he bought some range cattle and developed a good-sized herd. He already had a band of several hundred horses, but they were stolen by the Crees in 1883. The raid occurred at sunset, but before dark several Pikuni friends of Kipp, including Little Dog, Little Plume, and Tail-Feathers-Coming-Over-the-Hill, were in hot pursuit of the thieves. They overtook them and a fight ensued. Three of the enemy were killed and two of the Pikunis were wounded. Most of the horses were recovered.

In 1886, Kipp sold Fort Conrad to James McDevitt. That same year, he joined Schultz in guiding a party of English bankers named Baring through the St. Mary country on a hunting and fishing trip. Baring Falls and Baring Creek on the Going-to-the-Sun Road were named by Schultz for these visitors. In 1888, Kipp also collaborated with Schultz in guiding four businessmen from Troy, New York, on a hunting expedition through parts of future Glacier National Park. The visitors called themselves the Four Trojans and published a book entitled *Sport Among the Rockies*, telling of their exploits.

According to Jack Holterman, author of *Place Names of Glacier/Waterton National Parks*, no one has been more closely associated with the history of Glacier than Joseph Kipp. While this may be an overstatement, Kipp did collaborate in the 1880s with Schultz in guiding distinguished individuals on hunting and fishing expeditions in the St. Mary country. In the early 1890s, he took an interest in the gold prospecting that was going on in the heart of the future park. On the latest U.S. Geological Survey map, Mount Kipp and Kipp Creek are shown near the north end of West Flattop Mountain. Neither appeared on the original 1911 survey map, but "Kipp Cabin" was shown in the same general area.

Kipp was known to have built a cabin in this area for use by those doing assessment work on the various mining claims owned by a group he belonged to. Each of the claims had a name, such as Akamina, Alpine, Blackfeet, Glacier, Humboldt, International, Northern Light, Pumpelly, and Saskatchewan. There is no record that Kipp or his associates did any of this assessment work personally.

In 1894, Kipp hired two characters named Joe Cosley and J. H. Wallerback, also known as Porcupine Jim, to assess claims for him. The pair reportedly arrived on horseback via the Belly River and Ahern Pass and made themselves comfortably at home in the Kipp cabin while carrying on their work. All went well for a few weeks until they returned one evening to find the cabin and all their supplies and belongings burned.

This necessitated a four-day round-trip to Lake McDonald to replace their food, coats, and blankets. After a few more days of work, a heavy storm covered the ground with three feet of snow, forcing them to quit working. They struggled down the valleys of the Waterton River and Kootenai Creek until at last they reached a cabin belonging to Kootenai Brown. There is no record of whether they returned, but Kipp and his associates apparently abandoned their efforts to find gold in the area. As in 1868, when Kipp, Wrenn, and Thomas had prospected the entire eastern foothills of the Rockies, Kipp's efforts as a gold seeker were highly unsuccessful.

Schultz recalled that when he came to Montana as a youth, Kipp took him under his wing and taught him the ways of the frontier. "He was more than a brother to me," Schultz wrote later. "To him I owed the happiest years of my life." He went on to say that Kipp enjoyed the complete trust and confidence of everyone, including such prominent people as Charles and William Conrad, who each year gave the North West Mounted Police money to pay the Indians of Alberta an annuity of five dollars each. The total was always more than $100,000, and Kipp was always the man who carried it across the several hundred miles of lonely plains between Fort Benton and Fort Macleod.

According to Schultz, Joseph Kipp was the real leader of the Pikunis from the buffalo days to the time of his death. In all matters of tribal welfare, the chiefs came to him for advice, and they invariably followed it. In 1887, largely through Kipp's efforts, the tribe got $1.5 million in exchange for part of its reservation. It was by no means his fault that much of that sum was frittered away.

One of the acts of an early Montana Legislature was the unanimous passage of a bill granting Joseph Kipp full citizenship. He had not asked for the honor; it came to him as a surprise and was proof of the high esteem in which he was held throughout the region.

In his later years, Kipp lived on his ranch near the town of Blackfoot in Glacier County. He died unexpectedly on December 10, 1913, and was buried beside his mother, Earth Woman, at Browning. The news of his death came as a tremendous shock to Schultz, who was in California. Only a few days earlier, he had received a cheerful letter from Kipp, promising that he would meet Schultz in 1915 at the exposition to be held in San Francisco, and then they would return to Montana together. The letter was signed "Kipah, Mastwun'opachis" (Your elder brother, Raven Quiver).

6

James Willard Schultz

The Pikuni Storyteller

The well-known author James Willard Schultz thrilled young readers in the early 20th century with tales of the Wild West and life among the Indians. His books dealing with Glacier National Park provided such good publicity that the Great Northern Railway invited him to visit the park regularly at the railway's expense. *Courtesy of the James Willard Schultz Society*

James Willard Schultz was born in Boonville, New York, to well-to-do parents on August 26, 1859—less than two years before the outbreak of the Civil War. His parents were Frances and Philander Bushrod Shults, as the name was then spelled.

His father was of German extraction. The house in which James was born and raised still stands, bearing a plaque which identifies it as a New York State Historic Landmark.

From childhood, Schultz loved the outdoors, a passion which his father understood and appreciated. The elder Schultz arranged for two competent men to take his son into the nearby Adirondacks on camping and hunting trips. The boy became a skilled camper and an excellent shot.

Although James was rather precocious, he did not do well in school in his earlier years. At Sunday school, he questioned biblical legends, such as the one about Jonah and the whale, and soon he dropped out permanently. At public school, he earned a reputation as a troublemaker who resisted schoolroom discipline. So his parents withdrew him and had him privately tutored. He and his father struck a bargain: James could go on mountain outings if he applied himself to his books. After his father's death, his guardians continued the arrangement.

Because of his skill in shooting game and handling firearms, James was sent to Peekskill Military Academy on the Hudson River. Eventually, his parents hoped to send him to West Point. At Peekskill, he did well in history and English, and he became editor of the school paper. However, there was little about military life, particularly its discipline, that appealed to him. He continued to look forward to vacations, when he could enjoy his hunting and fishing trips to the mountains and could renew a boyhood friendship with a lad named C. Hart Merriam.

Young Schultz also developed a taste for music. Under his father's tutelage, he learned to play the violin. While at Peekskill, he would go to New York City whenever possible on weekends and stay at the Fifth Avenue Hotel, where he had often stayed with his parents. Then he would attend all the concerts and operas he could. He also would spend occasional hours at the hotel bar, where he could talk with men of experience.

His New York visits became so frequent that the headmaster at Peekskill put a limit on his off-campus leaves.

Following his junior year at Peekskill, Schultz was invited to spend the summer vacation with his uncle, Benjamin Stickney, who was the lessee and operator of the Planters Hotel in St. Louis, a hostelry famous for its catfish and crystal. It was a rendezvous for plantation owners and their families and for many important Westerners, such as Pierre Chouteau, Isaac Baker, and Charles and William Conrad.

Schultz soon discovered the Missouri and Mississippi Rivers, and he spent considerable time along the levees watching the loading and unloading of the great riverboats. Whenever he could, he talked with the captains or pilots about buffalo country and life and adventure in the Northwest. Before long, he wired his mother for money to enable him to make a trip by steamboat to Montana.

It took about 40 days to reach Fort Benton, the head of navigation on the Missouri. Schultz greatly enjoyed his journey up the treacherous river, traveling on the *Far West* as far as Bismarck, North Dakota, and completing the trip on the *Benton*. On arrival in Fort Benton, he was entranced by the sights of the frontier town, with its interesting mix of traders, trappers, and Indians.

Schultz had brought letters of introduction for several townspeople, which he presented on visits his first day in town. But his most important contact—one that was to change the course of his life—was with Joseph Kipp, a man some 10 years older than himself. In making the rounds with Kipp, he also met a man called Sorrel Horse, who invited Schultz and Kipp to his lodge to have dinner. Before the evening was over, young Schultz had been invited by both Kipp and Sorrel Horse to join them in their respective ventures in Montana.

Schultz chose to go with Sorrel Horse because he was leaving the next morning to trade with a band of Pikuni Indians. The trip would give the young newcomer a chance to ride horses and perhaps shoot buffalo. As it turned out, he was able to do some of both, as well as to learn a little of the Pikuni language. He spent much time with Sorrel Horse's half-Indian son, Wolverine, who was about Schultz's age. At the request of his friend, he even helped to abduct a Gros Ventre girl with whom Wolverine had fallen in love.

When Schultz returned to Fort Benton later that year, he found Kipp busily assembling supplies to trade with the Pikunis at their winter location, which the chiefs had decided would be in the open valley of Cow Creek, a small tributary of the Missouri. There, they expected to find plenty of buffalo and other big game, as well as reasonably mild weather.

Among those assembled at Cow Creek for the winter was Hugh Monroe, who had come west in 1815 to live with the Indians. With him were several of his family, including his grandson, Billy Jackson, just returned from service as an army scout in the Indian wars. Schultz had heard of Monroe, and he sought him out at once to become better acquainted and to learn more of his experiences.

Schultz was also attracted to Jackson, only three years his senior, and to Apsi (Arrow), a full-blooded Indian about their age. During the winter, the three of them had a number of interesting adventures together.

When Christmas arrived, old Hugh Monroe, a good Catholic, asked his wife and daughters to provide a special feast, to which Kipp, Schultz, and other friends were invited. Not long after Christmas, Schultz grew lonesome for home, and he returned to upper New York, where he spent six or eight weeks in the Adirondacks hunting panthers. In an 1880 magazine article, he told of killing three of the "varmints" while at a camp operated by Jack Shepard and Ed Arnold.

When Schultz rejoined Kipp at Cow Creek, he found that the trader had had only a fair season, taking in 2,000 buffalo robes and about the same number of other skins. When they returned to Fort Benton to settle accounts with the wholesaler there, Schultz learned with some surprise that Kipp had been given an opportunity to acquire Fort Conrad, a trading post of considerable size built in 1875 on the Marias River. Kipp urged Schultz to become a partner in the venture, but the latter thought it best to continue as an employee since he was a minor and still expected to return to Boonville.

The move to Fort Conrad, about 70 miles northwest of Fort Benton, was made in September 1878. Spending the winter there was a pleasant and rewarding experience for young Schultz, who became well acquainted with two women who were important to Kipp. One was his mother, Earth Woman, daughter of the great Mandan chief, Mah-to-to-pah. The other was her close friend and constant companion, Crow Woman.

There were rumors that the great buffalo herds were diminishing. With this in mind, prominent Pikuni chiefs met with Kipp in the summer of 1879 to discuss the trading plans for the coming winter. Based on reliable word that there were still plenty of buffalo in the area near the Judith River, Kipp agreed to build a trading post on the Judith if the Pikunis would winter there.

That winter on the Judith was a happy one for Schultz, who shared a cabin with Kipp and came to know him very well. However, the trading season came to an abrupt end when the Indians were ordered back to their reservation by the United States Army on charges that the tribe had been killing the cattle of a nearby settler.

Kipp decided to build another post for the winter of 1880–81 at Carroll, and among those who set up camp in the vicinity of the post were the Siksikas and Kainahs, both branches of the Blackfeet Confederacy from Canada. Later, a thousand Crees and a hundred families of Red River French *metis* under Louis Riel joined them. The Pikunis did not come because of the presence of their great enemies, the Crees.

The year proved to be a great one for Kipp. A Boston buyer gave him a check for $29,229.11 for his buffalo robes, while other buyers purchased his stock of other hides, smoked buffalo tongues, dried buffalo meat, and pemmican. This prosperity convinced Kipp to keep the post open for another year. When winter came, the Crees were still there, but most of the Kainahs and Siksikas had decided to return to Canada to take advantage of a treaty under which the government would pay five dollars to every resident member of the two tribes. Riel's *metis* remained, but Riel himself left for Canada without paying $700 he owed Kipp.

That was to be Kipp's last season at Carroll. It was only a fair one, although his 2,130 buffalo robes sold for $7.35 each. A representative of Charles Conrad bid on everything else Kipp had to sell. In July 1882, the post at Carroll was abandoned, and Kipp and Schultz sailed back to Fort Benton on the steamboat *Helena*. Never again would traders trade in the Indian camps of Montana.

Schultz and Kipp both deeply regretted the passing of the camp-trading era. Its demise coincided with the end of Schultz's first five years in Montana—years that he would later say were the happiest of his life. They were years spent almost entirely with Indians, speaking mostly in the Blackfeet tongue. Except for Kipp, his close friends were members of the Pikuni tribe.

During those five years, Schultz acquired an Indian name, Apikuni, which meant "Spotted Robe." The name was bestowed upon him by Chief Running Crane, a noted Pikuni warrior, in recognition of his bravery on the war trail and as a token of the chief's friendship.

During his first two years among the Indians, young Schultz gave little thought to romance or to members of the opposite sex, since there were no single white women on the frontier. One evening, as he was visiting his good friend Talks-With-the-Buffalo, the latter said, "Why don't you take a woman?" Schultz was taken aback by the question and could only give a lame response.

A few days later, however, young Schultz spotted a likely looking teenager among the young women of the tribe, and he asked Kipp what could be done about making her his woman. Kipp delegated the matter to his wife, Double Strike Woman, who soon had the deal arranged. Schultz could have the girl without having to give her family any horses or other customary items of value; all he had to do was to agree to treat her well. In other words, the girl's widowed mother gave her consent, pleased that her daughter would have a husband who was not only young and white, but attractive with good prospects.

No further rites or formalities were required, and Double Strike Woman arranged suitable quarters for the couple in one of the log cabins at Fort Conrad. Schultz was 20 and the girl 15. Her name was Mutsi-Awotan-Ahki, meaning Fine Shield Woman, but Schultz gave her the pet name of Natahki.

It was that same autumn that Kipp, with the assistance of Schultz, set up his trading post on the Judith River, far down the Missouri. Schultz worked there and at Carroll, Montana, for most of the next three years, and both places were considered too dangerous for wives. So Schultz did not often get to see Natahki, who lived with her mother at Robare.

At about the time of his 21st birthday, in August and September 1880, Schultz took time off to visit his mother in

Boonville and to sign papers relating to his father's estate. Natahki feared he would never return, but during his brief visit to Boonville Schultz realized how much he missed and loved his wife. He hurried back to Montana, and she was overjoyed to see him.

On February 18, 1882, while Schultz was at Carroll, his son was born. Schultz named him Hart Merriam in honor of his boyhood friend, C. Hart Merriam. An uncle gave him the name Lone Wolf, which the child eventually preferred to use.

While Schultz spent most of his time at the trading posts immersed in hard work, he also found time occasionally for recreation and adventure. His companions on these occasions were always Pikunis, such as Takes-Gun-Ahead (Eli Guardipee), Eagle Head, Heavy Breast, and Many-Tail-Feathers. Often their adventures involved the hunting of buffalo or grizzly bears.

One day while at Carroll, when the buffalo were becoming scarce, Schultz and Guardipee rode out on their fast buffalo horses, each armed with a rimfire, .44-caliber repeating carbine. Sighting a herd at the head of a long coulee, the two men charged into it and turned their horses after the cows they wanted—fat ones with rounded hips and rumps. Schultz shot six cows before his horse tired. Guardipee kept riding, and when he returned he had bagged 18 cows with 18 shots, a feat never equalled as far as Schultz knew.

On another occasion, Schultz was invited to join a party of about 30 men planning to raid the horses of the Assiniboines, eternal enemies of the Pikunis. The adventure lasted about three weeks and ultimately was successful, although unexpectedly so. The men surprised an enemy war party of Crees and, in a brief encounter, killed nine men and captured 63 horses without losing a man of their own.

After Kipp sold Fort Conrad in 1886, Schultz and Natahki built a cabin near the Two Medicine River on the Indian reservation, where they continued to live and raise livestock for more than 15 years. Schultz began building a business as a guide and outfitter.

In October 1883, Schultz and a party of six camped at the foot of Lower St. Mary Lake. They found an alkali lick at the base of a cliff just below the north end of a mountain that Schultz called Flattop. There they saw seven white goats and shot two of them. For the next few days they hunted around camp, and they went home without visiting the upper lake.

In 1884, Schultz returned to the St. Mary country with other friends and spent 21 days hunting, fishing, and exploring. With three of his associates, he rode along the northwest side of Upper St. Mary Lake to a point where they could see a glacier in the distance. In the meantime, other members of the group made trips up the Swiftcurrent Valley as far as the falls. The party also caught 92 whitefish, which tipped the scales at 232 pounds. Before Schultz and his party left the lakes, several other local parties arrived, including a camp of Pikuni Indians under Chief Yellow Fish.

In the summer of 1888, Schultz brought Natahki and their six-year-old son to the St. Mary lakes, where they spent much time boating and fishing on the upper lake. That fall, Schultz and Jack Monroe, another white man who sometimes assisted him as a guide and who also had a Pikuni wife, built a cabin near the foot of Upper St. Mary Lake and spent part of the winter there. For a time they were visited by two Indian friends, Ancient Man and Tail-Feathers-Coming-Over-the-Hill, who wanted to do some hunting. One day while Schultz and Tail-Feathers were resting after butchering a ram they had killed, the latter admired an imposing mountain across the lake. They discussed it and agreed that the name Schultz proposed for it, Going-to-the-Sun Mountain, was an appropriate one.

In early 1885, Schultz sent an article about the St. Mary lakes, entitled "To Chief Mountain," to a weekly publication called *Forest and Stream*. The article so interested the magazine's editor, George Bird Grinnell, that he wrote to Schultz to ask if Schultz would take him to the St. Mary country the following September to do some hunting. Schultz obtained Kipp's approval for a leave of absence and told Grinnell he would.

Grinnell turned out to be not only the first, but also the most frequent and appreciative of Schultz's outfitting clients. He also turned out to have interests other than hunting. When he arrived in September 1885, Schultz and a French halfblood named Yellow Fish took him to a pleasant spot near the upper end of the lower lake, where they found game to be scarce. Grinnell killed one ram with a lucky shot, and when he returned triumphantly to camp with the story of his exploit, Schultz promptly named the mountain where his good fortune had occurred Singleshot.

The party spent two days on horseback in the Swiftcurrent Valley, traveling as far as the falls, in which Grinnell was disappointed. A few days later Grinnell bade Schultz goodbye and started for the East.

In 1887, Grinnell paid a second visit to the St. Mary country, along with a friend from Santa Barbara, California, named George H. Gould. Schultz and Jack Monroe served as their guides. The weather was poor and Grinnell succeeded in bagging only two female mountain goats and a lynx. But after Gould left for home, Grinnell decided to explore the glacier that now bears his name.

With a week's supplies packed on two small mules, Grinnell, Schultz and Monroe succeeded in reaching the glacier and exploring it. While on the ice, Grinnell shot a magnificent ram from a distance of 200 yards. He also named the glacier, the little lake below it, and the pyramid-like mountain north of it after himself. He named Mount Gould for his Santa Barbara friend; Mount Allen for Cornelia Seward Allen, the sister of William H. Seward III; and Mount Wilbur for E. R. Wilbur, Grinnell's associate on the editorial staff of *Forest and Stream*. Lieutenant John H. Beacom, who spent a few days in the valley with the Grinnell party, gave a mountain north of Swiftcurrent Falls Schultz's Indian name, Apikuni.

Grinnell next returned to the St. Mary region in the fall of 1891, choosing as companions William H. Seward III, grandson of Abraham Lincoln's secretary of state, and Henry L. Stimson, who would later serve as secretary of war under both Theodore and Franklin Roosevelt and as secretary of state under Herbert Hoover. Their principal objective was to explore the upper St. Mary Valley, particularly the large glacier at its head. Billy Jackson assisted Schultz in guiding the party.

After four hard days of travel, the adventurers reached the glacier and explored it, camping near it for a time before returning to their original camp near the foot of the upper lake. It was a trip on which several names were conferred: Seward Ridge for William H. Seward III; Mount Stimson for Henry L. Stimson (the peak is now known as Mount Logan); Mount Jackson, the third highest peak in what is today Glacier National Park, for Billy Jackson; and Mount Reynolds for Charles E. Reynolds, longtime managing editor of *Forest and Stream*.

Blackfoot Glacier and Blackfoot Mountain were named for the Indian tribe. Gunsight Pass was named after the V-shaped sight on a rifle, as were nearby Gunsight Mountain and Gunsight Lake. Fusillade Mountain was named following an incident in which those in camp heard a volley of shots from the direction in which Seward and Stimson were hunting. Yet, the young men returned to camp with only one goat.

In 1886, three members of the English banking family of Baring came to the St. Mary country for a hunting trip guided by Schultz and Joe Kipp. The men arrived in September and hunted and fished in the area of Upper St. Mary Lake, each succeeding in killing both sheep and goats. Schultz named Baring Creek, Baring Basin, and Baring Glacier for his party; however, the U.S. Geological Survey map of Glacier National Park indicates that Baring Glacier has become Sexton Glacier. In lieu of Baring Basin, the latest survey map gives us Baring Falls.

In August and September of 1888, four citizens of Troy, New York, calling themselves the Four Trojans, came to the St. Mary's region for a hunting expedition conducted by Schultz, Kipp, and a third guide. They spent three or four weeks, mostly in the Cut Bank and St. Mary areas, and they killed, among other game, two grizzlies and a large bull elk. On returning home, they had the story of their experience published in a book entitled *Sport Among the Rockies.* Schultz never wrote anything about them or their expedition, and when he was shown a copy of the book, he insisted that their story was greatly exaggerated.

For Schultz, 1902 was an unusual year in that it marked the first and only time he ever served as a guide west of the Continental Divide. His client was Emerson Hough, a well-known writer whom Grinnell had urged to visit and write about the region. When Hough arrived in February 1902, Schultz and Billy Jackson took him via the Great Northern Railway to Nyack station on the west side of the future park. In temperatures as low as 30 degrees below zero and snow as deep as 10 feet, they spent an interesting but frigid 10 days. Conditions were not conducive to hunting most of the time, but Hough finally killed a large ram.

When Hough returned the following autumn with his wife and a friend, Jackson was unavailable, and Schultz arranged for a man named Joe Carney to help him guide the party. The group visited the Two Medicine and Cut Bank Valleys, the St. Mary lakes, and the beautiful Swiftcurrent Valley.

In November 1901, Schultz and Natahki made a boat trip down the Missouri River. It became the subject of a serial that appeared in *Forest and Stream* during the spring of 1902. During the trip, Natahki developed what appeared to be heart trouble, and she died several months later. Her loss was a bitter blow to Schultz.

Despite his grief, Schultz agreed to serve as a guide for Ralph Pulitzer, the son of famed journalist Joseph Pulitzer. When young Pulitzer wanted to shoot a ram in violation of Montana's game laws, Schultz collaborated with him, although Pulitzer killed four when Schultz thought he only meant to kill one. When authorities discovered the violation, Pulitzer was arrested, prosecuted, and fined. A warrant was issued for Schultz's arrest, but he fled first to North Dakota and later to California.

Schultz spent some time in San Francisco and then in Chowchilla, California, where he worked for an oil company. He had begun work on a book, *My Life as an Indian*, and he eventually finished it in Arizona, where he had gone to improve his health. While living with James Alexander, superintendent of the Pima Indian School, he met Dr. James Walter Fewkes, who was engaged in archaeological work at the Casa Grande ruins. He later devoted some time to assisting Fewkes in his excavation.

While ill and hospitalized in Phoenix, Arizona, Schultz read several issues of the *Los Angeles Times* and was impressed by the paper's sympathetic policy toward the Indians of Southern California. When released from the hospital, he went to Los Angeles and got a job as literary editor for the *Times*. In the meantime *My Life as an Indian* had been published, first as a serial in *Forest and Stream* and then in book form.

Unaccustomed to living alone in a big city, Schultz became so lonesome that he advertised in *Heart and Hand* magazine for a wife. After rejecting one applicant, he accepted a second named Celia Belle Hawkins, and they were married in early 1907. Although their friends could see they were not compatible, Celia was a good cook, which seemed to hold the marriage together.

In 1909, Schultz was reunited with his son, Lone Wolf, who had also gone to Arizona for his health and who later came to Los Angeles to attend school at the Art Students' League. He lived for a time with his father and stepmother, but Celia became so jealous that he went elsewhere. In 1913, Schultz had a cabin built high in the White Mountains of Arizona—a shooting lodge where the Schultzes spent much time.

In retrospect, Schultz's flight from Montana became a turning point in his life, because it obliged him to turn his hand to a different calling—one that was to bring him fame, if not fortune, and a welcome back to his beloved St. Mary/Swiftcurrent country. During his absence, the area had become a national park, and he would return as a visitor and camper. But his notoriety as an author also paved the way for his return as an important non-paying guest to the park's hotels for the next 15 summers. The hotels were operated by the Great Northern Railway, and because Schultz represented a potential advertising asset for the park, he became friends with the company's president, Louis W. Hill.

When Schultz returned to the park in 1914, he went to Hill with a unique idea: He would invite some of his Blackfeet friends to camp with him throughout the park, and he would learn from them the Indian legends concerning each place they visited. Then he would put the legends together into a book. Hill agreed to underwrite the entire project, which made it possible for Schultz to return the next summer to arrange three gatherings of his Indian friends for the summers of 1915, 1922, and 1925.

Among the 33 guests at the first two-month gathering were Eli Guardipee, Tail-Feathers-Coming-Over-the-Hill, and Yellow Wolf. The latter two were uncles of Schultz's first wife, Natahki.

The free camping party began in the Two Medicine Valley, rich in the Blackfeet lore that Schultz would need for the book he planned to write. Each evening around the campfire, he would ask some of his Indian friends to tell of the dramatic events that had taken place in that locale in earlier days. The mention of Trick Falls, for example, served as a cue for Tail-Feathers to tell about Running Eagle, the Blackfeet warrior maiden whose Indian name, Pitamakan, was the Blackfeet name for the falls.

After Two Medicine, the party camped for a few days each in the Cut Bank Valley, on the Milk River in the Blackfeet Reservation, at the foot of Upper Lake St. Mary, and finally, in early September, in the Swiftcurrent Valley beside the lake of the same name. They lingered at this beautiful spot until September 10, when they broke camp and the Blackfeet returned to their reservation. Schultz returned to Southern California to write *Blackfeet Tales of Glacier National Park*, and it was published the following year.

As a result of a similar reunion hosted by Schultz for his Indian friends in 1922, *Friends of My Life as an Indian* was written. *Signposts of Adventure* was published in 1926, following a camping trip the previous year with "the older men of the Pikuni and their families upon the shores of Two Medicine Lodges Lake."

Each summer, beginning in 1915, Schultz made a pilgrimage to Montana, where he and Celia spent much time in Glacier National Park. His books dealing with the park provided such good publicity that the Great Northern Railway invited the couple to stay at the park's hotels free, and sometimes it provided them with free transportation to and from Southern California. However in 1924, Schultz bought an automobile, and from then on the couple made their annual trip to Montana by car. The rest of the year was spent in California or Arizona.

Schultz and his wife made their last trip together to the park in 1927. Schultz liked to attend the Indian ceremonies at Browning and elsewhere, but these were of no interest to Celia, who stayed in a park hotel until he returned. When she learned that he had attended a 10-day Indian dance ceremony in the Belly River region with another woman, she became very unhappy, and their relations deteriorated until they parted forever in May or June, 1928. Schultz eventually filed for a divorce, which was granted September 5, 1930. Under the terms of a subsequent settlement, Celia was granted a half interest in all royalties accruing from Schultz's books published on or before that date.

The woman with whom Schultz had attended the Belly River ceremonies was Jessica Donaldson, a professor of English at Montana State College. She was deeply interested in Indians and was likewise interested in Schultz because of his great concern about Indian affairs and welfare. When Schultz separated from Celia, he went to live with or near Jessica in Bozeman, which caused college authorities to request her resignation. When she resigned near the end of the 1928–29 school year, she and Schultz spent the summer with the Blackfeet Indians in Alberta, Canada.

They continued to live together for the more than two years before he finally divorced Celia. In the meantime, the Great Depression had begun, and Jessica was unable to get a job. During the winter of 1928–29, she and Schultz collaborated in writing *The Sun God's Children*, the research for which she had done the previous summer in Calgary, Alberta. When the summer of 1929 ended and the couple had no home to which to return, they accepted an invitation from Lone Wolf, to whom Schultz had given the Arizona cabin, to spend the autumn months there. Jessica and Schultz's son and daughter-in-law got along well together.

In 1930–31, Jessica earned a master's degree in anthropology from the University of California at Berkeley, with financial assistance from her brother, Gilbert. Schultz lived with or near her, and the couple finally drove to Winnemucca, Nevada, to get married April 27, 1931. They hoped that some of their troubles were behind them and that they could now look forward to a more pleasant way of life. Unfortunately for the newlyweds, things were destined to get worse before they got better.

For more than three years after their marriage, Jessica was unable to obtain employment because of the Depression. Schultz injured his back as they were driving to Montana—an injury that proved to be serious. It took him through a series of hospitals as well as treatment by a succession of doctors.

The painful disability and its complications crippled him for the rest of 1931 and much of 1932. The couple were fortunate to be able to spend part of each of the next three or fours years with Schultz's son and daughter-in-law at the Arizona cabin. They finally returned to Berkeley, where the back ailment was cured.

When employment conditions failed to improve, the Schultzes returned to Bozeman, where they had a fishing cabin on the Madison River. They apparently were living there when Jessica got a federal job at Choteau, Montana, in September 1934. By this time, Schultz was 75 years old and no longer able to write well.

After a short time, Jessica was transferred to Browning, Montana, where she was under the jurisdiction of the Indian Service. For the Schultzes, the move to Browning was a turn for the better. It brought him back to a community and people with whom he was familiar. It also allowed them to help their Indian friends in need, since part of Jessica's job was to dispense federal aid.

Jessica remained at this post until 1940, when she was transferred to a similar position at the Wind River Indian Reservation at Fort Washakie, Wyoming, a reservation which was half Arapaho and half Shoshone. She was successful here, as she had been at Browning with the Blackfeet, in convincing the Indians to begin an arts and crafts program to help them become at least partially self-supporting. In the meantime, Schultz, now in his 80s, was disabled much of the time by illness or injury. While in Denver, Colorado, where Jessica was pursuing a master's degree in social work, Schultz fractured a hip.

While the Schultzes were in Wyoming, Schultz was unable to do any writing and was barely able to carry on a cursory correspondence with a few friends. Jessica, 28 years younger than her husband, continued her work with the Indians until 1953, when she retired. She continued thereafter to keep busy with various projects until her death in July 1976. In 1961, she was given an honorary doctor's degree in letters by Montana State University in recognition of her outstanding work with the American Indian.

Although his formal education was limited, James Willard Schultz wrote his first piece for publication at the age of 21. In the next 15 years, he wrote a number of articles and stories for *Forest and Stream*, a newspaper/magazine to which he subscribed. Some of these attracted the attention of the publication's editor, George Bird Grinnell.

Grinnell's interest in the Blackfeet tribe and the St. Mary country grew along with his relationship with Schultz. He wrote *Blackfoot Lodge Tales* in 1892, borrowing heavily from Schultz. As a matter of fact, he only wrote the book after tying in vain to get Schultz to do so.

Schultz did not write his first book, *My Life as an Indian*, until 1907, and it was a great success. Nonetheless, several years passed before he finally realized that the writing of Indian-white adventure stories was his forte. About 1911 or 1912, he made a connection with Houghton Mifflin, which was to be the sole publisher of his works for nearly 30 years. When he was nearly 50 years old, he began writing steadily, turning out two and sometimes three books a year until there were 37 altogether.

All but 10 of these volumes were also serialized, most of them in either the *Youth's Companion* or the *American Boy*, where they became popular reading matter for the youth of this country from 1912 to 1932. He also wrote five long serials that did not become books.

In addition to *My Life as an Indian* and the other 36 books published during his lifetime, four collections of his stories were put together and published in book form posthumously. These were *Blackfeet and Buffalo*, 1962, *Floating on the Missouri*, 1979, *Why Gone Those Times?*, 1974, and *Many Strange Characters*, 1982. All were published by the University of Oklahoma Press.

While no figures are available on the number of Schultz books sold to date by Houghton Mifflin, it has been estimated that the number may exceed two million. It is believed that *My Life as an Indian* alone may have accounted for a half a million or more sales, including hundreds of thousands sold after 1956 by other publishers. Some of Schultz's books were published and sold in Europe.

A strange phenomenon of the publishing world is the James Willard Schultz Society, which came into existence in 1976, nearly 30 years after his death. The pages of its quarterly publication are filled with articles and other information contributed by Schultz aficionados and others. The society even has triennial two- or three-day conventions—always held in Glacier National Park, Schultz's old stomping ground.

Along with James Fenimore Cooper, Schultz has been considered one of the foremost writers on the subject of Indian adventure. Most of his stories were directed at a younger group of readers who found his stories in the *Youth's Companion and American Boy* so fascinating that they could hardly wait for the next installment. However, his stories also made a deep impression on older readers and were received with great acclaim by such literary critics as William J. Long, author of *Outlines of American Literature*; Professor Verne Dusenberry, of the English department of Montana State University; Stanley Vestal, able western writer for the Dallas News; J. Donald Adams, of *The New York Times*; and Hubert V. Coryell, whose articles appeared in various magazines during Schultz's lifetime.

Particularly enthusiastic about Schultz's work was Keith J. Seele, who served as editor of *Blackfeet and Buffalo*. His introduction to the volume is an exercise in superlatives. Grinnell, who wrote the introduction for *My Life as an Indian*, describes it as "a remarkable story" and speaks of it in the highest terms.

When a survey of the works of Montana authors was recently conducted by Professor Harry W. Fritz for *Montana, the Magazine of Western History*, James Willard Schultz and A. B. Guthrie, Jr., both ranked high, with nine titles each.

Schultz has enjoyed a loyalty from his readers which continues in spite of defects in his work which many seem to overlook. His more perceptive readers charge him with two principal faults: (1) That in dealing with dates and other facets of Montana history he was frequently inaccurate; and (2) that he tiresomely repeated certain episodes and stories in many of his books, although the versions in each often varied widely. His story of the christening of the St. Mary lakes, for example, appeared in six of his books, but without being the same in any two.

The editors of his posthumous books were well aware of these faults, and they warned their readers against relying on Schultz's version of history. Yet neither of these defects seemed to have a significant effect upon his reputation; nor did they hurt the sale of his many books.

Schultz was honored to be considered a member of the Blackfeet tribe. Throughout his life, whenever situations arose in which his Indian friends needed a champion, Schultz became their self-appointed spokesman, and he was an effective one. In two different periods of privation among the Blackfeet, he did everything possible to relieve their problems. He tried to help the Hopi Indians when they were being persecuted for following their native religious ceremonies. His greatest achievement on behalf of the red man was the formation and leadership of "The Indian Welfare League," which was able to win full citizenship for the Indian in 1924.

It was a matter of common knowledge among his friends that Schultz was fond of alcoholic beverages. Today he would probably be regarded as an alcoholic, although his third wife thought his addiction to whiskey was, at times, a help in his writing. But she alone knew of his addiction to morphine. When he injured his back in 1931, the doctors he visited prescribed the drug to relieve the intense pain. Eventually, Schultz realized he was addicted, and only after a year's difficult struggle, the loyal assistance of his wife, and the dedicated efforts of two physicians in Berkeley, California, was he able to rid himself of the problem.

While Schultz enjoyed hunting throughout his life, he also loved pets and had many of them—some from the wild kingdom, others domestic. At different times he had as pets a wolf, a coyote, a beaver, and a young mountain goat. Schultz and his third wife had a series of cats and dogs which afforded them much pleasure and sometimes accompanied them wherever they went.

Despite the fact that Schultz lived to a ripe old age, he suffered from ill health during much of his life. He had heart and lung infections from time to time that were incapacitating, and after he attained his allotted three score and 10 years, he became injury-prone.

In addition to the spinal injury of 1931 and the complications resulting from its treatment, he fractured his left leg and right arm when he fell at home in October 1942. Perhaps his worst injury was sustained in September 1944 in Denver, when he fell and fractured his right hip. He had to have surgery, which left his left leg two inches shorter than his right.

Obviously, Schultz was no stranger to hospitals. At various times he was a patient in Arizona, California, Montana, Nebraska, Colorado, Wyoming, and even Alberta, Canada. At least twice he underwent surgery, and his health had so far deteriorated that during the last seven years of his life, he was unable to do any writing, much as he wanted to.

After his hip injury, Schultz's attention span became shorter and shorter, and his eyes began to bother him. This was followed by the onset of progressive coronary disease, and he suffered a fatal heart attack June 11, 1947, on an afternoon when four inches of snow fell on the Wind River Reservation in Wyoming, where he was residing at the time. The Blackfeet have a saying that it is sure to storm when a chief passes.

Schultz had wanted to be buried in Montana, so his family laid him to rest at the old burial ground of Natahki's family, near her uncle, Red Eagle, and other friends of his youth. Later, they decided to disregard his request that his grave be unmarked. So many requests came from the readers of his books that the Indian agent at Browning prevailed upon his wife and son to have a suitable marker made and set in place. Lone Wolf designed a simple stone to symbolize his father's life with the Blackfeet.

7

George Bird Grinnell

Father of Glacier National Park

A man of many talents, George Bird Grinnell led the campaign to set aside Glacier National Park after discovering the area's attractions in 1885. Calvin Coolidge once commended him with these words "You have done a noteworthy service in bringing to the men and women of a hurried and harried age the relaxation and revitalization which comes from contact with Nature." *Courtesy of Glacier Park Archives*

George Bird Grinnell was born September 20, 1849, in Brooklyn, New York, to George Blake and Helen A. Lansing Grinnell. Among his ancestors were five colonial governors and Betty Alden, the first white woman born in New England.

Another ancestor was president of Yale University from 1740 to 1766.

Grinnell's early years were spent in Audubon Park on Manhattan Island. His father had purchased a building site there from Mrs. John James Audubon, widow of the famous artist and ornithologist. The house he had erected served as the family home for 50 years. When the Grinnells first moved in, Mrs. Audubon was running a small school for her grandchildren and some of the neighbors' children. George enrolled and learned from her about birds. When he caught a bird in a crab net, she identified it for him as a red crossbill. Before he was old enough to own a gun, he borrowed one and shot a ground dove, a species which had never before been sighted so far north. His early experiences in Audubon Park may have helped Grinnell to develop his interest in natural history.

Grinnell attended Churchill's Military School in Sing Sing (now Ossining), New York, completing his studies in 1866. He traveled extensively in Europe before entering Yale University, where he received a bachelor of arts degree in 1870, a doctor of philosophy degree in 1880, and an honorary doctor of letters degree in 1921. In 1870, after graduating from Yale, young Grinnell toured the West with an expedition headed by O. C. Marsh, a renowned paleontologist who had set out to collect vertebrate fossils. Grinnell was only 20 years old, his head filled with Mayne Reid's tales of the Wild West, when he learned of Marsh's proposed expedition. "I felt that I had no qualifications for a position on such an expedition," he wrote later. "However, after much pondering, I mustered up courage, called on Professor Marsh, and asked if I could in any way attach myself to his party. I found him far less formidable than I had feared."

Marsh not only accepted Grinnell but asked his help in securing other young men, most of whom, like Grinnell, went along with the hope of finding adventure.

138

The party of a dozen men and boys left New Haven, Connecticut, in late June and was gone nearly six months. It traveled through several Western states and territories and brought back valuable collections, including the extraordinary series of fossils that was to form the basis of Professor Marsh's book *Dinocerata*. Grinnell was fascinated with everything he saw on the journey—vertebrate fossils, rocks and minerals, trees and flowers, birds and big-game animals, and especially Indians. He met Brigham Young in Utah and visited San Francisco, the Yosemite Valley and the redwood forests of California. For the rest of his life, he would return again and again to the West for stimulation and pleasure.

In 1872, Grinnell and a friend, Luther North, joined a camp of 4,000 Pawnee Indians for their summer buffalo hunt, an event that helped to crystalize his interest in the American Indian. Years later, his first book was entitled *Pawnee Hero Stories and Folk Tales*. It was followed by *Blackfoot Lodge Tales*, *The Story of the Indian*, *The Indians of Today*, *The Fighting Cheyennes*, *The Cheyenne Indians*, and 16 other books on Indians of the early West.

In the late spring of 1874, General Phil Sheridan wrote Professor Marsh to tell him that a military expedition was going to the Black Hills of Dakota that summer and to advise him that he could send someone along to collect fossils if he wished. Marsh asked Grinnell to go, and Grinnell asked North to be his assistant. The assignment promised excitement, since the Black Hills were then a region of mystery.

General Sheridan instructed Grinnell to report to Colonel William Ludlow, chief engineer of the Department of Dakota. So Grinnell and North took a Northern Pacific train to Bismarck, North Dakota, just across the river from Fort Abraham Lincoln. Since the expedition's departure date was still three weeks away, Grinnell and his companion were assigned quarters at the post. In the meantime, they were entertained occasionally at the home of General George Armstrong Custer, who delighted in relating his hunting exploits.

The expedition was scheduled to begin toward the end of June and end about two months later. Its members started over the roadless prairie, crossing the Cannonball, Grand, and Moreau rivers and later the north fork of the Cheyenne. Game was plentiful, and there was no shortage of fresh meat. When the command neared the south end of the Black Hills, General Custer ordered the expedition to halt for a day while his chief scout, Charley Reynolds, delivered a number of dispatches to the Union Pacific Railroad. Riding chiefly at night and hiding by day, Reynolds made the trip safely, although on a number of occasions he saw Indians pass his hiding places.

Shortly after the command turned north for the return trip, Colonel Ludlow asked Grinnell to prepare a report on the birds and mammals of the Black Hills region for the secretary of war. The expedition reached Fort Lincoln about September 1, and Grinnell returned home.

Grinnell's work must have pleased Colonel Ludlow, because in 1875 he asked the Yale graduate to accompany him as naturalist on a reconnaissance through parts of Montana and Wyoming, including Yellowstone National Park, then only three years old. Ludlow was unable to pay anything or even to furnish railroad transportation, but he did offer to provide Grinnell with everything he needed while in the field.

Ludlow's party proceeded by train to Bismarck and then boarded the steamboat *Josephine* for the trip to Carroll, Montana. A cavalry unit escorted it through the Judith Mountains to Fort Ellis, and from there it continued on to Yellowstone Park. During the survey, Grinnell became concerned about the wanton destruction of game on the frontier. In his report to Ludlow, he wrote:

It may not be out of place here to call your attention to the terrible destruction of large game, for the hides alone, which is constantly going on in those portions of Montana and Wyoming through which we passed. Buffalo, elk, mule deer, and antelope are being slaughtered by thousands each year, without regard to age or sex, and at all seasons. Of the vast majority of animals killed, the hide only is taken. Females of all these species are as eagerly pursued in the spring, when just about to bring forth their young, as at any other time.

It is estimated that during the winter of 1874–75 not less than 3,000 elk were killed for their hides alone. Buffalo and mule deer suffer even more severely than the elk, and antelope nearly as much. The Territories referred to have game laws but, of course, they are imperfect and cannot, in the present condition of the country, be enforced. Much, however, might be done to prevent the reckless destruction of the animals to which I have referred, by the officers stationed on the frontier, and a little exertion in this direction would be well repaid by the increase of large game in the vicinity of the posts where it was not unnecessarily and wantonly destroyed . . . The general feeling of the better class of frontiersmen, guides, hunters, and settlers is strongly against those who are engaged in this work of butchery, and all, I think, would be glad to have this wholesale and short-sighted slaughter put a stop to. But it is needless to enlarge upon this abuse. The facts concerning it are well known to most Army officers and to all inhabitants of the Territory. It is certain that, unless in some way the destruction of these animals can be checked, the large game so abundant in some localities will ere long be exterminated.

Thus was Grinnell's philosophy of conservation formulated. He loved hunting—or outdoor sportsmanship as he called it—but he detested useless slaughter of wild game.

After the expedition with Marsh in 1870, Grinnell worked under the professor's direction preparing osteological materials for the Peabody Museum at Yale University. In 1874, he was promoted to a permanent position as assistant in paleontology, and he remained for several years at this post, working chiefly on vertebrate fossils between his trips west. By 1880, the confining work had undermined his health; he resigned the job and returned to New York.

In the spring of 1876, Grinnell was invited to accompany an army expedition to subdue the Indians in Montana. However, he was so busy with work on his doctoral degree, his duties at the Peabody Museum, and some writing he was doing for *Forest and Stream* that he passed up the opportunity. It was just as well. The man who invited him was George Armstrong Custer and, had Grinnell accepted, he probably would have been a victim of the massacre on the Little Bighorn. The Indians would have killed the young man who was to become their staunchest defender over the next half century, and the nation would have lost a first-rate historian and folklorist, as well as an outspoken advocate of the national park system and a protector of wildlife.

Grinnell's writing career began in 1876, when he became natural history editor of the New York publication, *Forest and Stream*. Later he would serve as its editor and then owner until 1911. Through the magazine, he was able to voice his ideas about the conservation of wildlife—ideas ahead of their time.

At the invitation of Luther North, Grinnell spent part of the summers of 1877, 1878, and 1879 at a ranch in western Nebraska, where William F. Cody and Luther's brother, Frank North, had gone into the cattle business. At first, the only shelter Grinnell and his friend could find was a pair of tents, but eventually a comfortable sod house was built. The duo did a great deal of hunting. In the summer of 1879, Grinnell also went hunting in North Park, Colorado, where deer, elk, mountain sheep, and bear were plentiful. Grinnell wrote an account of the trip, entitled "A Trip to North Park," for *Forest and Stream*.

In the summer of 1881, A. H. Barney, president of the Northern Pacific Railroad, asked Grinnell if he would like to see the country through which the railroad was being built. The line had been completed as far as Yellowstone National Park. Grinnell accepted the invitation and decided to go by way of the Union Pacific to San Francisco and then by boat to Victoria, British Columbia. From Nanaimo, British Columbia, he and his companions traveled 600 miles north by canoe to Butte, Jervis, and other inlets along the coast of British Columbia.

Returning to Portland, Oregon, Grinnell traveled east via the Northern Pacific Railroad to Spokane, Washington, then only a small village at the end of the track. By team, sailboat, pack train, and stage, he made his way to Deer Lodge, Montana.

When the railroad reached Yellowstone, the park became more easily accessible to visitors, including some who saw its possibilities as a resort area. A corporation was formed—the Yellowstone Park Improvement Company—and it secured from the assistant secretary of the interior conditional leases for 10 plots of 640 acres of land in the park and the use of park timber for construction.

Grinnell had been through the park in 1875 with Ludlow's expedition, and he had some understanding of how the public could best enjoy it. In the autumn of 1882, he launched an attack through *Forest and Stream* against the proposed monopoly and its ripoff of park facilities. Fortunately, the park had friends who were alert to what was being attempted.

In 1893, Grinnell sent into Yellowstone Park the first expedition ever to visit in winter. The expedition gathered information that led to the capture of a poacher who had been killing buffalo in the park. Reports of conditions there were spread via the newspapers to all parts of the country, and they led to the enactment of the Park Protection Act in May 1894. In the early 1920s, an even more alarming proposal threatened the park when irrigation interests proposed to dam Yellowstone Lake. Again, Grinnell issued a clarion call to friends of the park, with the result that its defenders, both in and out of Congress, rallied to the cause, and the plan failed.

In 1886, Grinnell founded the Audubon Society to curb the practice of killing small birds so that their bright plumage could be used on women's hats and dresses. He announced the idea in the February 11 issue of *Forest and Stream*, saying the goals of the society would be "to prevent, so far as possible, (1) the killing of any wild birds not used for food; (2) the destruction of nests or eggs of any wild bird; and (3) the wearing of feathers as ornaments or trimming for dress."

As a journalist, a member of the American Ornithologists' Union, and a lover of wildlife, Grinnell had clear ideas about the dangers inherent in wholesale destruction of bird life. But it was obvious that resolutions by scientific societies would accomplish little—partly because they would reach so few people and partly because the average American had not the slightest interest in what scientific associations resolved. It seemed to Grinnell that the only way to encourage change was to appeal directly to women about the wearing of feathers and to teach children about the beauty, charm, and utilitarian value of birds.

From the very beginning, the press expressed its approval of the Audubon Society. The Forest and Stream Publishing Company distributed great quantities of literature about it.

144

Local secretaries were selected in towns all over the land. The members of the bird-preservation committee of the American Ornithologists' Union lent powerful aid. Such eminent citizens as Henry Ward Beecher, John G. Whittier, John Burroughs, Oliver Wendell Holmes, Bishop Henry Potter, and a multitude of others commended the idea. In two or three years, the society had members scattered all over the country. Membership was free, and expenses were borne by Forest and Stream Publishing Company.

In February 1887, *Audubon* magazine was established, but it had to be discontinued at the end of 1888 because it was too expensive. After a lull that lasted a decade, public interest in the society revived and the movement achieved the success it is known for today.

Grinnell first discovered the attractions of the St. Mary/Swiftcurrent region of northwestern Montana in the autumn of 1885, after reading a description of the area written by James Willard Schultz for *Forest and Stream*. In September, he traveled with Schultz to the St. Mary country, and he was so impressed that he wrote a 14-installment story about the experience. The series was called "To the Walled-In Lakes,"[6] and he wrote under the pseudonym "Yo."

The trip was significant. His love for the region, which he would visit again and again, would prompt him to lead a successful campaign to make it part of a national park. Some would even propose calling it Grinnell Park.

Grinnell arrived at the Blackfeet Agency in early September 1885 to spend three weeks near the St. Mary lakes. He traveled with James Willard Schultz, whose Blackfeet name was Apikuni, and a French half-blood whose Indian name was Yellow Fish. By team and wagon, they headed northwest to Lower St. Mary Lake, a hundred miles away. When they reached the Cut Bank River, after traveling 17 miles, they were able to procure saddle horses for Grinnell and Schultz, and they reached the lake three days later.

The outset of the expedition was inauspicious: The weather poor and game was scarce. Nonetheless, Grinnell was able with a single lucky shot to kill a bighorn sheep. When he triumphantly returned to camp and told the story of his adventure, Schultz announced that the mountain where the kill had been made should thereafter be known as Single-shot Mountain. While in the vicinity, the party visited a band of Kootenai Indians and were amazed when its chief, Back-Coming-in-Sight, rang a little bell for vespers and joined his flock in prayer.

The party had difficulty circling the west shore of Upper St. Mary Lake on horseback, although Grinnell found the scenery magnificent. He was disappointed in Swiftcurrent Falls, but did get a distant glimpse of the glacier which would later bear his name.

When the group returned to the agency, Schultz arranged for Red Eagle, an old Indian medicine man, to stage the elaborate Bear Pipe ceremony, asking in his prayers for pity on those present. The next morning Four Bears, the camp orator, bestowed upon Grinnell the name Fisher Cap.

Grinnell returned to the Montana mountains two years later, and Schultz again served as his guide along with a white man named Jack Monroe. The second trip resulted in a series of 18 articles for *Forest and Stream*, entitled "The Rock Climbers." This time Grinnell invited a friend, George H. Gould, of Santa Barbara, California, to share the trip with him.

Since the previous trip, the Canadian Pacific Railway had been completed from coast to coast. As a result, Grinnell and Gould were able to meet in Lethbridge, Alberta—Grinnell arriving from Montreal in the east and Gould from Vancouver in the west. Schultz had to drive about 200 miles with team and wagon to pick up his clients and bring them to the trip's starting point on Lower St. Mary Lake.

Although it was only the latter part of September, an early snowstorm began. Game again proved to be scarce, even on the mountainsides. The men paired off, Gould with Monroe and Grinnell with Schultz, and they tramped all over the region day after day. In the almost three weeks they spent there, Grinnell bagged only two female goats. They hung the meat in a tree near their tent, which did not stop a lynx from getting to it. Grinnell killed the tree-climbing prowler.

Gould had to return to California October 25, and so Monroe escorted him back to Lethbridge. After they had left, a friend of Schultz, Lieutenant John H. Beacom, visited while on vacation from his army post. Grinnell told him of their plan to spend a week traveling up the Swiftcurrent Valley and asked him to join them. They moved their camp to a point near the foot of Lower St. Mary Lake and cached their boat and supplies. By the time Monroe returned, they were packed and ready to go.

The party established a base camp just below Swiftcurrent Falls, opposite a mountain to which Beacom gave Schultz's Indian name, Apikuni. Then they concentrated on finding a route to the glacier; two of them traveled along the west side of Swiftcurrent Lake while the other two moved along its east side, where they found an old Indian trail. They progressed as far as possible along the second lake before they ran out of time and had to return to base camp.

Beacom had to leave, but the other three men packed three days' worth of supplies and gear on their two small mules and returned to the ascent, reaching what is now Grinnell Lake the first day. At daybreak the next morning, they reached the glacier, which they spent much of the day exploring. While on the ice, Grinnell killed a magnificent ram at a distance of 200 yards. Three days later, they returned to their camp at the foot of the lower lake. Schultz took Grinnell back to Lethbridge. En route, they were stopped and searched by Canadian mounted police, who mistook them for liquor smugglers.

During the trip, the party named a number of topographical features, including Grinnell Glacier, Grinnell Lake, and Mount Grinnell. Grinnell himself conferred the names of Mount Gould for his Santa Barbara friend; Mount Allen for Cornelia Seward Allen, granddaughter of William H. Seward, Lincoln's secretary of state; and Mount Wilbur for E. R. Wilbur, Grinnell's associate on the editorial staff of *Forest and Stream.*

When Grinnell planned another trip to Montana in 1891, he brought along two remarkable young companions, William H. Seward III and Henry L. Stimson. The former was a grandson of Lincoln's secretary of state, while Stimson was an attorney who would return the following year to make the first ascent of Chief Mountain by a white man and who would eventually serve as secretary of state under President Herbert Hoover and secretary of war under the two Roosevelts. Assisting Schultz as guide was Billy Jackson, grandson of Hugh Monroe. Jackson had served as a scout to General Custer during the 1874 expedition to the Black Hills and so had met Grinnell before.

During this visit, Grinnell's principal objective was to explore the glacier above Upper St. Mary Lake and the adjacent country. So the five-man party headed up the lake's western shore. Progress was slow the first day, because the terrain was rugged, and a packhorse stumbled on the trail and rolled down a slope. The men spent three days struggling through heavy brush and over fallen timber before they reached a pleasant campsite only a few hundred yards below the glacier.

Here the party spent an enjoyable fortnight, exploring the glacier, climbing the surrounding mountains, and hunting goats, sheep, and ptarmigan. The men even reached the summit of a pass over the Continental Divide (Gunsight Pass), from which they could see a small lake (Ellen Wilson Lake).

Grinnell had three other objectives in mind during this trip: He wanted to finish mapping the St. Mary/Swiftcurrent area, gather data for the book *Blackfoot Lodge Tales*, to be published in 1892, and prepare a report describing to the public the territory he covered.

Grinnell and his party again bestowed many names upon the mountains and other scenic features of the territory. Mount Jackson was named for Billy Jackson; Mount Stimson for Henry L. Stimson (the peak is now known as Mount Logan and another has been named for Stimson); and Mount Reynolds for Charles E. Reynolds, managing editor of *Forest and Stream*. Blackfoot Glacier and Mountain were named for the Indians of the region. Gunsight Pass was named for its notch-like resemblance to the sight on a rifle, and the same name was given to nearby Gunsight Lake and Mountain. Fusillade Mountain got its name when the men in camp heard a volley of shots from the mountainside, where Seward and Stimson had gone to hunt. They returned with a single goat to the teasing of their friends.

Following his 1891 explorations, Grinnell completed a surprisingly accurate "1885–1892 Sketch Map of the St. Mary's Lake Region."

While Stimson and Seward returned to their Eastern homes after the four-week outing, Grinnell lingered for another month on the Blackfeet reservation, visiting with the Indians and compiling, with Schultz's assistance, the material which on his return to New York he would incorporate into the 1892 book, *Blackfoot Lodge Tales*.

Grinnell's story of the 1891 expedition got wider readership than his past efforts for *Forest and Stream*. He apparently had begun to have a broader appreciation for the region and was beginning to think it should be set aside as a scenic and recreational preserve fur the general public, not just for a few hunters and wealthy campers. So he sent an article about the trip to *Century* magazine for publication. For some reason, it was not published until September 1901, under the title "The Crown of the Continent." This may have been just as well, since the area had gone through a mining boom in the interim, which, by the time the article was printed, had finally petered out.

After its belated publication, the article was hailed by many as the opening volley in the campaign to make the St. Mary country part of a national park. The article did not actually propose national park status for the region, but its laudatory language made a strong case for the designation. Because of this article, Grinnell has often been referred to as the Father of Glacier National Park.

Grinnell was a man who used superlatives sparingly, but he showed little restraint in describing the future park in his *Century* article:

No words can describe the grandeur and majesty of these mountains, and even photographs seem hopelessly to dwarf and belittle the most impressive peaks. The fact that it is altogether unknown, the beauty of its scenery, its varied and unusual fauna, and the opportunity it offers for hunting and fishing and for mountain climbing, give the region a wonderful attraction for the lover of nature.

In 1895, President Grover Cleveland appointed Grinnell to a commission working with the Blackfeet Indians to fix a fair price for the land that lies between the Lewis Range and the present western border of their reservation. Grinnell's efforts brought the Blackfeet half a million dollars more than the other commissioners wanted to approve. During negotiations, Grinnell took the other commissioners to the head of St. Mary River. He made a hasty trip to the same region in 1897, and in the following year he climbed Blackfoot Mountain.

Grinnell's good deeds and sage counsel endeared him to members of the Blackfeet tribe, and he was beloved by Chief White Calf. In January 1903, White Calf caught pneumonia while visiting Washington, D.C., and he died January 29. In a letter written two days later, Grinnell voiced his sorrow:

A good many years ago (in the early 1890s) when in the big lodge in the center of the circle, at the Medicine Lodge in the ceremonial at which all the chiefs were present, he made me stand up by his side and told me that he now transferred to me the care of his people, and henceforth I should be the head of the tribe. I have tried hard to deserve the confidence he put in me then and later, but I have often failed.

In an attempt to earn his friend's trust, he made many trips to the agency for council meetings and powwows and to give advice.

Grinnell was also a longtime friend of Theodore Roosevelt, who shared his love of the outdoors. Both men came from similar backgrounds, and both went West as explorers, naturalists, and big-game hunters. At a dinner at Roosevelt's home in 1887, the Boone and Crockett Club was founded, and Grinnell later served as its president. In fact, during the half century he was a member of the club, Grinnell served on every committee and held every office except treasurer. When he retired in 1927, he was made honorary president for life. Originally, Roosevelt and Grinnell edited club publications together, but when Roosevelt was elected to the White House, Grinnell continued the work alone.

Although in a brief autobiographical note written for *American Men of Science* Grinnell described himself only as an anthropologist, he actually wore many other hats during his long career. He was naturalist, sportsman, conservationist, paleontologist, mountain climber, cowboy, explorer, geographer, cartographer, zoologist, ornithologist, editor, publisher, and author. He was a man interested in all the wonders of the world, but, like his friend, Roosevelt, he was keenest about the outdoors.

In 1898, Grinnell had a chance to serve on an extraordinary expedition to investigate Alaska. It was sponsored by the president of the Union Pacific Railroad, E. H. Harriman, who chartered a vessel and assumed all of the expenses of the ambitious trip. The expedition left Seattle, Washington, May 31 and returned about two months later.

Harriman had given C. Hart Merriam, chief of the U.S. Biological Survey, the job of deciding whom to invite, and the list included every outstanding American scientist and Alaskan expert. No one declined, although one man had to postpone his wedding to participate. The final guest list included 23 of the country's top scientists representing a dozen fields, plus three artists, two photographers, two physicians, two taxidermists, and one chaplain. Of course, Harriman and his family were included.

While in Alaska, Grinnell met Edward S. Curtis, a Seattle photographer. When the cruise was over, Grinnell suggested that Curtis accompany him to the Blackfeet reservation in Montana. There, Curtis photographed the Indians, and his pictures turned out so well that he spent much of the next 30 years photographing tribes throughout the United States. Two thousand of these pictures were incorporated into his masterpiece, *The North American Indian.*

Between 1889 and 1918, Grinnell produced more than a score of volumes on Indians, Western history, hunting, camping, and conservation. He was also a frequent contributor to the *Journal of American Folklore, American Anthropologist, Harper's, Century, Scribner's,* and others. His subjects ranged from the myths of the Plains Indians to tribal customs and traditions.

Among Grinnell's most popular books were several for children: *Jack Among the Indians*; *Jack, the Young Cowboy*; *Jack in the Rockies*; *Jack, the Young Explorer*; *Jack, the Young Canoeman*; and *Jack, the Young Trapper.* They were written when Grinnell was in his 50s, primarily, he said, for his nieces and nephews. The hero was a western lad who visited the West for adventure, as the author had done in his youth.

Grinnell's books, particularly those on the Cheyennes, were the product of a lifetime of observation, personal interviews, and research into the Indians' way of life. So detailed were his descriptions of dress, courtship, the place of women in the tribe, implements of war, hunting methods, games and amusements, religion, and accounts of battles that his books have long been valuable reference books. For example, his *Blackfoot Lodge Tales*, originally published in 1892, was republished by the University of Nebraska Press in 1962. It was so popular that successive printings were issued in 1965, 1968, and 1970.

In 1925, when President Calvin Coolidge presented Grinnell with the Theodore Roosevelt medal for promotion of outdoor life, the laconic New Englander summed up Grinnell's career in a single paragraph:

You were with General Custer in the Black Hills and with Colonel Ludlow in the Yellowstone. You lived among the Indians, you became a member of the Blackfoot tribe. Your studies of their language and customs are authoritative. Few have done as much as you, none has done more, to preserve vast areas of picturesque wilderness for the eyes of posterity in the simple majesty in which you and your fellow pioneers first beheld them. In the Yellowstone Park you prevented the exploitation and, therefore, the destruction of the natural beauty. The Glacier National Park is peculiarly your monument. As editor for 35 years of a journal devoted to outdoor life, you have done a noteworthy service in bringing to the men and women of a hurried and harried age the relaxation and revitalization which comes from contact with Nature. I am glad to have a part in the public recognition which your self-effacing and effective life has won.

The Roosevelt medal was conferred upon Grinnell in the eighth decade of his life, and Grinnell's many admirers were pleased to see him receive the well-deserved, though belated, acknowledgement of his accomplishments.

Grinnell was instrumental in founding the New York Zoological Society, and he served as one of its trustees. He helped found and served as director of the American Game Association. He was active in the National Park Association, and in 1925 he succeeded Herbert Hoover as its president.

Among the other clubs to which Grinnell belonged were the Union Club, the University Club, the Century Club, the Rockaway Club, the Mayflower Descendents, the Society of Colonial Wars, the Authors Club, the Explorers Club, the Narrows Island Club of North Carolina, the Cosmos Club, and the Washington Biologists Field Club. He was also a member of the American Society of Mammalogists, the New York Academy of Sciences, the Archaeological Institute of America, the New York Genealogical and Biographical Society and the Phi Upsilon Fraternity.

Grinnell was a trustee of the Hispanic Society of America and of the National Association of Audubon Societies, as well as a fellow of the American Association for the Advancement of Science, the American Ethnological Society, the American Geographical Society, the American Museum of Natural History, and the American Ornithological Society.

On August 21, 1902, Grinnell married Elizabeth Kirby Curtis, a Boston widow. She was an enthusiastic photographer who accompanied him on most of his travels after their marriage. They camped with the Blackfeet on one occasion, living in a tipi, studying the Indians' customs, and listening to their stories. In 1926, they visited Grinnell Glacier for the last time.

In 1906, Grinnell purchased a 200-acre country estate in Connecticut, where he and his wife spent most weekends. Occasionally they hunted ruffed grouse and woodcock in the swales and quail in the fields, for Grinnell always owned hunting dogs.

In 1928, Grinnell's last major work was published. Entitled *Two Great Scouts and Their Pawnee Battalion*, it was a salute to Frank and Luther North, who had introduced him to the Pawnee Indians more than half a century before. Grinnell died 10 years later on April 11, 1938, at the age of 88.

Someone once said of him:

Aside from Grinnell's prophetic vision, his forthrightness, his scholarship in the fields of zoology and Indian ethnography, and the drive that empowered him to carry so many causes to successful conclusion, his outstanding personal characteristic was that of never-failing dignity, which was doubtless parcel of all the rest. To meet his eye, feel his iron handclasp, or hear his calm and thrifty words even when he was a man in his ninth decade was to conclude that here was the noblest Roman of them all.

8

Hart Merriam Schultz

Blackfeet Artist

Hart Merriam Schultz, commonly known as Lone Wolf, the part-Blackfeet son of writer James Willard Schultz, turned to art as his medium of expression. Through painting and sculpture, he brought the West alive for countless people who appreciated, as one art critic said, his "uncompromising realism ... his sincere treatment of the human form." *Courtesy of James Willard Schultz Society*

Hart Merriam Schultz, more commonly known as Lone Wolf, was an only child, the son of James Willard Schultz and his Blackfeet wife, Natahki. He was born February 18, 1882, at Robare Crossing on Birch Creek, Montana, close to Joe

Kipp's trading post. Natahki was staying with her mother at the time, because her husband was in Carroll, Montana, helping Kipp to trade with the Indians.

The naming of Blackfeet children was considered the father's prerogative, but since Schultz was absent, others thought they should step into the breach. A priest named the child Thomas, but Natahki's uncle, a medicine man named Red Eagle, gave the boy the name Lone Wolf[7] in keeping with a vision he had had. When the baby's father returned home, he was unhappy with both names and chose to call the child Hart Merriam after his boyhood friend, C. Hart Merriam, who had become a noted physician and anthropologist.[8] Some of the Blackfeet thought the baby should be called Black Eagle, after his maternal grandfather, but young Schultz always used the name Lone Wolf.

Lone Wolf's early years were spent near Fort Conrad, at his parents' ranch on the Two Medicine River and at three different schools which he attended and despised. During those years, his grandfather, Yellow Wolf, taught him how to prepare and use natural colors and how to draw animals and people.

The first school Lone Wolf attended was at Fort Shaw; he and other Blackfeet children were taken from their parents and dragged there, their long braids were cut off, their buckskin clothes were replaced with white man' s clothing, and if they were heard speaking their native tongue, they were strapped with a leather belt. Later, Lone Wolf attended the new Catholic school at the mission on Two Medicine River. When the schoolmaster tried to punish Lone Wolf and another boy with a heavy wooden rule, they joined forces to beat him up, and Lone Wolf was expelled by the superintendent. He was delighted, and when he arrived home his surprised parents decided he could forgo school for awhile.

In his 12th winter, Lone Wolf's father enrolled him in the Willow Creek School on the reservation. His mother was unhappy to see him go, but his father was anxious that he receive an education. Here again, discipline was drastic. Finally, when the schoolmaster hit a boy with the handle of a pitchfork, Lone Wolf and several schoolmates piled onto him and gave him a beating. For this, they were all put in jail, and when Lone Wolf was released, his father decided he should come home for good.

Now a teenager, Lone Wolf found that life on the ranch along the Two Medicine was busy. His father was frequently away guiding wealthy Easterners through the region that was to become Glacier National Park. Consequently, he had to learn how to operate a cattle ranch, and, luckily, he had the help of his uncle, Last Rider, who became like a second father to him.

Ranch work left little time for painting. Nevertheless, Lone Wolf was able to sell his first watercolor to Jack Carberry, a clerk in Joe Kipp's store at Browning. Some 30 years later, Carberry returned the painting as a sentimental gift to Lone Wolf.

When James Schultz finally tired of the ranch and sold it to his friend, Eli Guardipee, Lone Wolf was forced to look for work as a cowboy and bronc buster.

As a young adult, Lone Wolf's defiance of authority continued to assert itself. Following the death of his mother, one of his cowboy cronies was Angus Monroe, a grandson of the legendary Hugh Monroe. According to Angus, Lone Wolf was at that time a wild young cowboy frequently in trouble with the law both on and off the reservation.[9]

Lone Wolf was mixed up in several horse-rustling cases. And once, when he and Angus rode into the wild railroad town of Cut Bank, just outside the reservation, they had little difficulty in buying drinks, despite the fact that in those days it was against the law to sell liquor off the reservation to anyone with Indian blood. Liquor was not permitted at all on the reservation.

The pair were enjoying themselves when Lone Wolf got into a fight with a white man who knew that Lone Wolf was wanted by authorities. When the fight broke up, the man sent word to law officers that Lone Wolf was in town. By this time, he and Angus had taken a hotel room and were preparing for bed. When they heard several horses ride up, they looked out their second-floor window and recognized the sheriff and his deputy. Lone Wolf jumped out a window in back, climbed onto his horse, and struck out for the reservation. There he was free from pursuit, because only federal officers had authority.

According to Angus, he and Lone Wolf traveled to many of the early rodeos held in the area and competed as bronc riders. They also rode together for a number of years on the big Indian Department roundups each spring and fall. Angus and his wife, Lily, were friendly with Lone Wolf and his first wife, a full-blooded Indian named Margaret Strong Woman. Margaret and Lone Wolf later divorced after the latter came down with tuberculosis. After he remarried, the Schultzes and the Monroes stayed in touch by letter, and they always saw each other when the Schultzes visited Blackfeet country.

Because of his lung condition, Lone Wolf was advised by doctors to seek a change of climate, and not long after his mother's death he headed for the Southwest where he would spend part of every year thereafter. In 1906, he took a job as a cowboy, horse wrangler, and guide at the Grand Canyon, continuing to paint whenever he could. While there, he met artist Thomas Moran, who recommended that Lone Wolf study at the Art Students' League in Los Angeles.

Lone Wolf had lost contact with his father after the latter's departure for the West Coast in 1903, and it was not until 1909 that they were reunited. He went to live with his father and attended art school in Los Angeles, but he could not tolerate the jealousy of his stepmother, Celia Hawkins. He moved on to study at the Chicago Art Institute for a time, but he found that he missed life in Montana. He returned to the West and resumed working as a cowboy.

In 1916, Lone Wolf went to work at the Galbraith ranch on the Milk River, not far from the Canadian border. Near the ranch, a construction crew was repairing the tracks of the Great Northern Railway. The camp foreman, Eli Tracy, maintained a home in Cardston, Alberta, where his children could attend school. His daughter, Naoma, who was in high school, often heard from her brother, who also worked with the crew, about the camp and the work. He also mentioned a young cowboy named Lone Wolf, who was a spectacular rider and a good artist.

One day Naoma persuaded her father to take her with him to the camp in the hope of meeting this remarkable horseman. When her father introduced him, she was impressed by his good looks and soft-spoken courtesy. Lone Wolf thought she was the prettiest red-cheeked girl he had ever seen. They were infatuated with each other, and in the days that followed they managed to meet several times.

Five months later, Lone Wolf arranged to meet Naoma at the edge of the construction camp. They rode 65 miles to the ranch of his uncle, Last Rider. The next day they rode on to Cut Bank, where they were married by a justice of the peace. The marriage lasted 54 years.

During the summer of 1914, Lone Wolf had spent some time at his father's mountain cabin in Arizona. The pair had selected a site on which the elder Schultz promised to have a cabin built for his son. In 1916, the cabin was completed, and Lone Wolf and his new bride moved in. From then on, the couple spent part of every year there, and in the mid-1920s, James Schultz gave the entire property to them. Over the fire-place in the main cabin, they hung a painting of the Grand

Canyon which Lone Wolf had given to Naoma as a wedding present.

In 1917, Lone Wolf held his first art show in Los Angeles. The *Los Angeles Times* carried the headline "Vance Thompson Discovers Wonderful Indian Artist, An Artist With a Vision." In the article, Thompson, who was the art critic for the Times, said in part:

> *It is a rare thing to discover an artist. I have seen the young painters pass in droves through the schools and salons of Paris, and in 20 years I can claim to have been the discoverer of only one great artist. Now I like to think that I have, at last, discovered another and he is an artist who has authentic vision, sincerity and a brush which is already capable of doing precisely the thing he wants it to. . . .*
>
> *Lone Wolf has courage . . . artistic courage which is the rarest of all. His strength as an artist is in his uncompromising realism . . . in his sincere treatment of the human form . . . in his intimate knowledge of the life he paints. You might call it quality, but whatever you call it, it is the one thing that keeps art alive, this man of the Blackfeet tribe has got it. He has got it. And to art lovers and painter folk I want to say one thing, there is a new artist coming up the trail and the name on him is Lone Wolf. His pictures are signed with a wolf's head.*

Collectors and enthusiasts of the Old West finally started to seek him out. During summers, Lone Wolf could be found on the east side of Glacier National Park at his St. Mary studio. In autumn, he would move to his spacious studio at Butterfly Lodge in Arizona, while in later years he would move to Tucson for the winter and spring. Charles Russell made several visits to the summer studio seeking advice on ethnological details.

In 1920, E. R. Yarnell of Florida saw Lone Wolf's paintings at Glacier National Park, and he brought them to the attention of his business associate, August Hecksher, of New York City. The latter, an ardent art collector, was to become one of Lone Wolf's devoted patrons. He arranged for the artist to hold his first eastern exhibition in New York City, and he bought all the paintings from the show. He also introduced Lone Wolf to the Babcock Galleries, which handled his work for years. With the New York show a sellout, Lone Wolf was besieged by reporters, and the city's newspapers lionized him.

Lone Wolf's work found its way into collections and museums of international importance. Among his early patrons were Mrs. Calvin Coolidge, Herbert Hoover, Owen Wister, Burton Holmes, Robert Colgate, H. S. Duryea, J. C. Kinney, and Dr. Philip G. Cole. He estimated near the end of his life that he had produced about 500 paintings.

The 1920s saw Lone Wolf venture into sculpture. August Hecksher purchased his bronze entitled *Camouflage* and donated it to Brookgreen Gardens in 1929. Only one cast was made of the *Buffalo Run*, which was purchased by Hecksher's son as a wedding present for his father. When Hecksher died, the bronze was purchased by Evelyn Walsh MacClean, of Washington, D.C. It is now in the collection of the Phoenix Art Museum in Arizona.

Many of Lone Wolf's sculptures were never cast in bronze, for the 1930s brought lean times and casting costs were high. One by one, the clay models were lost. *Riding High* and *Keeper of the Moons* were the only two pieces that survived in Lone Wolf's personal collection and, in 1967, they were cast in a limited edition.

Eventually, the years of bronc-busting—the bruises and the broken bones—began to take their toll. Arthritis set in, and

Lone Wolf's artistic ability gradually diminished until only a limited market existed for his work. Still, he stayed at the easel every day in his efforts to record the past.

Lone Wolf died February 9, 1970, in Tucson, a few days short of his 88th birthday. As he had requested, his ashes were buried June 19 in the grave of his beloved uncle, Last Rider, on the old ranch close to Cut Bank Creek that held so many happy memories.

On July 16, 1971, his widow, Naoma, accompanied by his adopted son, Paul Dyck, and Dyck's wife, Star, went to Browning, where the Give-Away Feast of the Blackfeet was held in Lone Wolf's honor. Hundreds of Blackfeet and visitors attended to see the photographs, paintings, and other memorabilia of Lone Wolf's life.

In retrospect, there were many similarities between the lives of Lone Wolf and his father. As youngsters, both were obstreperous students, resentful of school discipline, with the result that each left school early. Both led adventurous lives on the Montana frontier, and each narrowly escaped a brush with the law.

Both father and son suffered from health problems which led each, without the knowledge of the other, to Arizona. From there, both went to Los Angeles, where each scored his first major success in his field. Both returned to Montana and particularly to Upper St. Mary Lake, where Lone Wolf, like his father decades earlier, had a cabin. Charles Russell was a friend of both men.

As the years wore on, both men suffered from arthritis that hindered their work. Each died of progressive heart disease, after living about 88 years. Both died outside Montana but were buried in keeping with their wishes in the beautiful valley that each had for so long called home.

9
Charles Marion Russell
Cowboy Artist

Many of Charles Marion Russell's ideas for paintings originated at his log studio on the western shore of Lake McDonald. For almost two decdes he spent every summer there, tramping the quiet trails in search of inspiration or sitting at an easel on his porch, a few feet from the lake shore. *Courtesy of Montana Historical Society*

Charles Marion Russell was born in St. Louis, Missouri, on March 19, 1864, when the Civil War was raging and Montana was only a faraway territory on the frontier. His parents were Charles Silas Russell and Mary Mead Russell, and Charlie was the third of their six children.

The Russells were descended from early American stock. Charles Marion's great-great-grandfather was Silas Bent, who commanded a regiment during the Revolutionary War, and his great-grandfather of the same name was judge of the Court of Common Pleas as well as a signer of the first charter of St. Louis. The judge fathered a remarkable group of children, among whom were Charles and William Bent, who established Bent's Fort on the Sante Fe Trail.

Bent's Fort was the largest trading and outfitting center in the Southwest. The Bent brothers, raised in a well-to-do and socially advantaged family, introduced at the isolated fort many of the social amenities to which they had been accustomed in St. Louis, including good food, fine wines, and even a billiard table. Some of the West's best-known frontiersmen worked at one time or another at the fort, among them Jim Beckworth and Kit Carson, who was to become a brother-in-law of Charles Bent.

Charles Marion's grandmother, Lucy, was a sister of Charles and William Bent. At age 21, she married James Russell, a widower 20 years her senior. He had purchased 42 acres of land on the outskirts of St. Louis and in 1820 built a spacious home called Oak Hill. When he died in 1850, his widow took over management of the property, which included orchards, vineyards, gardens, slaves' quarters, livestock, and an extensive outcropping of coal. Under her capable handling, the family's business interests expanded and its real estate holdings grew. She brought Russell's father, Charles Silas, and her son-in-law, George W. Parker, into the profitable business of supplying coal to St. Louis and fireclay to the entire country.

Russell's father married Mary Mead, daughter of silversmith Edward Mead, whose reputation for fine work was well established in St. Louis. Following a long honeymoon in the East, they bought a home on Olive Street in St. Louis, but by the time their son was five, they had moved to the Oak Hill property. It was there, in the midst of a socially and culturally advantaged family, that Charles Marion Russell grew up.

Russell never liked school and seemed unable to apply himself. He spent much of his time drawing pictures of animals in the margins of his schoolbooks, and he was frequently punished for doing so.

Russell had a friend, Archie Douglas, who cooperated with him in a scheme to play hookey. Douglas composed notes to the teacher asking that Russell be excused from school while he visited an aunt. The ruse worked for seven weeks. Every morning Russell would take his books and ride to school. There, he would hide the books and spend the day at the waterfront or at the mule barns, perhaps watching the riverboats being loaded or unloaded or talking to the fur traders and plainsmen who were arriving from or departing to the great Northwest. But one day, as he was going to meet the carriage that would take him home from school, he saw his father coming. Instead of obeying his father's order to go home, Russell ran away for three days.

Determined that the boy should be educated so that he could take over the family business, his father sent him to a military school in Burlington, New Jersey. Russell did poorly and spent much of his time reading western novels by Ned Buntline. When he was caught, he was assigned to walk guard for hours carrying a wooden gun. During a midterm break, Russell refused to return to the academy.

Noting the youth's artistic tendencies, Russell's father enrolled him in art school and hired a private tutor to help him with his other studies. For awhile, Russell was happier with this arrangement and, under his tutor's guidance, read history and accounts of frontier life. But then the regimen of art school began to bother him and he withdrew. He worked three months for a farmer, hoping to raise enough money to go West. When his parents realized the seriousness of his intentions, they arranged for him to travel to Montana with a family friend, Wallis W. (Pike) Miller, who owned an interest in a sheep ranch on the upper Judith River in central Montana. They expected him to tire of the West in three months.

When Russell reached the sheep ranch, Miller gave him a job herding sheep. Russell hated sheep, and after three months he left the ranch with nothing but two horses and a couple of blankets. He was feeling discouraged when he met a mountain man named Jake Hoover, who took pity on Russell and invited the youth to his cabin. Russell ended up living with Hoover for the next two years, sharing the profits the mountain man made selling hides and meat.

Russell saved his money until he had enough for a trip to St. Louis; he did not stay long and was soon back in Montana. Virtually broke, he finally succeeded in getting a job as a night herder. He did well and participated in a huge cattle drive down to the railhead on the Yellowstone River. He continued to work as a cowboy in 1886–87, serving as a wrangler and night herder for the Bar R outfit.

That winter made bitter history for Montana cattlemen. It was the hardest they had ever seen, and it was immortalized by Russell in a postcard painting of a starving cow in a snowdrift, entitled *Waiting for a Chinook*. The postcard won him recognition, but it was a long time before he made money painting pictures.

Throughout Russell's earlier years in Montana, he came into only occasional contact with Indians, despite the fact they were numerous. Then, in 1888, Russell went to Canada to live with the Kainah tribe of the Blackfeet Confederacy. He learned to speak its language and also became proficient in the sign language common to all Western Indians.

After a few months among the Kainahs, Russell knew details of their customs, appearance, lifestyle, religion, and methods of warfare. He hunted with them and listened to their legends and lodge tales. He let his hair grow long and, because his cowboy outfit had become worn out, he adopted much of the Indians' garb.

He loved the Kainahs and was likewise loved and trusted by his new friends. His closest friend was Sleeping Thunder, the young son of a chief of the tribe. Sleeping Thunder urged Russell to forsake the path of the white man and marry one of the Indian women. He also gave him the name Ah Wah Cous, meaning Antelope, a name he carried through life.

As time passed, Russell made many friends among the Indians. Through their generosity, he collected Indian costumes, head-dresses, medicine bags, moccasins, and decorated ornaments. Each year, he took trips to the Indian festivals and gatherings, particularly those of the Blackfeet in Browning, Montana. The tribes always made him welcome by setting up a lodge of poles and buffalo hides for his use.

Indians were the subject of many of his paintings, such as *Medicine Man*, *Piegans*, *Wolf Men*, *Smoke Talk*, *Spoils of War*, *Signal Glass*, and *His Wealth*. The thorough knowledge he gained through his contacts equipped him to be a historian of the Indian on canvas.

After Russell's six-month sojourn with the Kainahs, he made his way back to the Judith Basin only to find that the old cow days were ending. Farmers and sheepmen were moving in and choking the open range. The cowmen detested these newcomers and their infernal barbed wire. From 1889 to 1892, Russell found intermittent employment with various outfits north of the Missouri River. In the meantime, his art was demanding more and more of his time. After spending some time in Great Falls, he returned to Chinook, Montana, and worked as a night herder; however, after a winter there, he again went south to Great Falls, dividing his time for the next two years between Great Falls and Cascade and spending it painting, modeling, loafing, and selling a picture when he needed money for food.

The year 1895 was an eventful one for Russell. One day he met his old friend, Ben Roberts, on the street in Cascade. Roberts invited him to dinner, Russell accepted, and they rode together toward the little house where Roberts lived on the bank of the Missouri. Soon after Russell arrived, he noticed a beautiful 17-year-old girl who was busy doing chores in the kitchen. Russell took off his Stetson as Roberts introduced him to the girl. Her name was Nancy Cooper, and as the months passed, Russell spent more and more time with her, until his friends began to spread rumors that the longtime bachelor was about to marry.

The rumors were true. The pair were married at the Roberts home September 9, 1896. He was 32 and she was 18. Russell realized that he now had a responsibility to earn a living. He began to devote more time to planning and executing his paintings, and his work steadily improved. He spent $75 converting a one-room shack with a lean-to kitchen into a presentable home.

Russell's bride soon took over the couple's financial affairs, including the sale of his paintings. After a year, they moved to Great Falls, and before long his paintings were commanding prices of three and sometimes four figures.

Russell's father visited the couple shortly after their move to Great Falls. Before leaving, he purchased lots and arranged for the construction of a modern home. In 1903, Russell had a log studio built nearby.

Russell enjoyed outings in the mountains during the summers. One of his favorite spots was in the Rockies not far from the Canadian line. There, on the western shore of Lake McDonald, he built a summer home to which he returned almost every year for the next two decades. He loved the profusion of wild game in this section of Montana, its romantic history, its crisp, clean air, its towering mountain peaks, its turquoise sky, and its great silences. It provided him with a respite from the summer heat that seared the Montana plains.

This log cabin became his studio. He devoted the morning hours to his art, beginning paintings that would be completed during the winters in Great Falls. Much of his work was done out-of-doors, tramping the quiet trails or sitting at his easel on the spacious porch of the cabin, a few feet from the lake shore.

The cabin was constructed in such a way as to preserve as many of the surrounding trees as possible, and the trail by which it was reached was a winding path with occasional log steps. Over the doorway was a kind of hood which served to protect a buffalo skull, the emblem of the camp and the inspiration for its name, Bull Head Lodge. In signing his work, Russell always drew a buffalo skull with his name.

As time went on and he added to the cabin, he invited special friends to spend time there with him and his wife. Afternoons and evenings were devoted to these guests, who were either close personal friends from his cowboy days or artists he had met on trips East. He enjoyed showing his friends the country he loved.

Russell ventured forth into other parts of Glacier National Park. In the summer of 1915, he trekked the trails of the region as part of a group led by Howard Eaton, a Wyoming rancher. Also in the party was novelist Mary Roberts Rinehardt, who wrote *Through Glacier Park: Seeing America with Howard Eaton*. In her book, she told of crossing some of the mountain passes, and she quoted Russell's comment upon arriving at the summit of one of them: "I'm getting right tired of standing in a cloud up to my waist."

Among Russell's many friends in the park area was Lone Wolf (Hart Schultz), the artist son of James Willard Schultz. During the years when Lone Wolf had a summer studio at St. Mary, Russell occasionally visited him to consult about Pikuni life.

Other close friends included Joe Kipp, a veteran of the Indian trading days whose mother was a Mandan princess. Kipp was a trusted adviser of the Pikuni tribe, and Russell liked to talk to him because of his wide experience and common sense. Once, Russell urged him to write a book about his people, their history and customs, as well as about his personal experiences—even offering to illustrate the book for him. Kipp declined, however, since he had no illusions about where the Indian stood in the white man's world.

Russell also knew Lone Wolf's father and Kipp's close friend, James Willard Schultz, his contemporary in central and northwestern Montana.

Russell always undervalued his work. At the beginning of his artistic career, he was satisfied with $10, $15, or $25 a picture. If no one seemed ready to buy, he would often give a painting away. But after his marriage, his work began to increase in value as well as quantity. He began to get requests for book and magazine illustrations, as well as shows and exhibitions. He exhibited at Montana state fairs and at the 1904 St. Louis World's Fair. After a showing at the 1912 Calgary Stampede, he was invited to a special show in Saskatoon, Saskatchewan, in honor of the prince of Wales. As a result, the future king of England became the owner of one of Russell's paintings depicting the Royal Canadian Mounted Police, entitled *When Law Dulls the Edge of Chance.*

Russell still managed to snatch brief respites from his work by heading for Jake Hoover's place, or to Johnnie Mathewson's ranch near the Highwood Mountains. At other times, he would go to the Lazy K Y Ranch to visit his friend Con Price and ride the horses reserved especially for his pleasure.

The Russells also made occasional trips to foreign countries. In 1906, Russell was commissioned by *Outing* magazine to do a series of illustrations in Mexico. The success of his Canadian and metropolitan shows brought an invitation to exhibit at the Dore Galleries on Bond Street in London in April 1914, where Russell's work was received with enthusiasm.

A friend urged the Russells to visit Paris before returning home from England. Charlie was opposed to the idea, but Nancy was anxious to see Paris and her will prevailed. The couple spent three days there, most of which Nancy devoted to shopping. Charlie had nothing but contempt for the Frenchmen.

The Russells had traveled from New York to the British Isles on the *Oceanic*, a ship which later went down during the first World War. Strangely enough, the same fate was met by the ship they chose for the return voyage—the *Lusitania*. On their eastward crossing, the ocean was very rough, and the Russells both became seasick. As Charlie put it, "The old Atlantic had no respect for size. This boat done the tango, hesitation waltz an' all the late snakey dances all the way across."

Russell had many friendships in Montana cow country, but perhaps the most intimate was with Con Price, a man five years his junior. Their acquaintance began in 1889 and ripened into a friendship that lasted almost 40 years. It was Con Price who "batched" with Russell in 1895–96, his last year of bachelorhood.

By 1899, Price had also married and had settled on a squatter's claim in the Sweetgrass Hills of Montana, four miles south of the Canadian border. The ranch, in addition to the basic claim of 360 acres, included some 3,000 acres of government land under fence. With limited capital, Price struggled hard to eke out a living, since he needed money to stock the ranch. On one of Russell's visits to the ranch, Price told him of his problems, apparently offering to make his friend a partner in return for much-needed capital.

In typical Russell fashion, Charlie told Price to figure out what the spread was worth, including the livestock, and he would invest an amount equal to half the estimated total. With that, a partnership was formed between the two cowboys. Price was able to build a herd of about 300 cattle, and he acquired about 60 horses. The Russells filed on land adjoining the Price ranch, and the firm of Price-Russell was established January 1, 1906.

The cattle brand of the partnership was the Lazy K Y, and the horse brands were the Three, reverse E, and the T brand. The latter, one of the oldest brands in Montana, was transferred to the partnership by Montana Governor Joseph Toole as a mark of esteem for Price and Russell. The cowboy artist's favorite horse at the ranch was Sandy, a gift from Price.

Russell's interest in the ranch gave him something he had always wanted—a place on the range where he could ride, sketch, and escape the city whenever he chose. He was a frequent visitor to Price's ranch house during the five years the two friends were partners. Whenever the Prices could get away from ranch duties, they visited the Russells in Great Falls. On these occasions, Russell and Price would hole up in the artist's log cabin studio to smoke and talk of their early cowboy days.

In 1911, Price sold the Lazy K Y—land, stock, equipment, brands, and all. Then, he went to Great Falls to settle accounts with his friend and partner. When he walked into the log cabin studio with the ranch books under his arm, Russell asked what the books were for, and Price told him he wanted to go over the partnership accounts with him. "Hell," said Russell, "burn 'em and give me a check. Your word's good 'nough for me."

One of the first books Russell illustrated was *The Story of the Cowboy*, by Emerson Hough, published in 1897 by D. Appleton and Company. For three paintings, he received $30. Less than 30 years later, a wealthy oil man paid him $30,000 for a mural painting. When Russell saw the check—and was convinced of its accuracy—he told his wife, "Why, Mama, that's dead men's prices."

During the intervening years, Russell's work appeared in 50 magazines, more than 100 art calendars, and 69 books. He also produced many pieces that never appeared in print, including about 70 bronze sculptures and literally thousands of pen-and-ink and pencil sketches and illustrated letters to friends—a prodigious output for anyone man. He is estimated to have produced about 2,000 paintings alone. Yet, he was sometimes called lazy, perhaps because he was apathetic when it came to doing anything but work at his easel or with his beeswax or modeling clay.

Of all his works, the color reproductions of his watercolor and oil paintings are best known. Millions of prints have been published of some 125 of his paintings. They have been household fixtures in the United States since the beginning of this century, and they are still in demand more than 60 years after his death. Several of America's largest calendar houses have specialized in Russell subjects. His color prints have made him the best known of all Western artists.

The first calendars to contain color reproductions of his paintings were published in the late 19th century. In 1905, he signed a contract giving Brown & Bigelow of St. Paul the option of selecting from his paintings a specified number of subjects for their line of calendars and color prints. Russell received $500 for each of the pictures reproduced, while retaining ownership of the original paintings. The cowboy artist who less than 10 years before had painted for "hotcakes-and-coffee" money had hit pay dirt.

Despite the fame and fortune he began to accumulate, Russell remained unchanged. He simply loved to paint; it was the joy of his life. Powerful and colorful as his works were, he always spoke of them with a half-apologetic air of nonchalance. He really did not sense their value, because to him the canvas, the brushes, and the pigments were only a means of expressing feelings he could not put into words. His wife once grew concerned that Russell might run out of ideas, but he reassured her by saying that no man ever lived long enough to paint all the pictures he had in mind.

Russell's works commanded exceptional prices, considering the vast number of them in existence. The reason must be that, great as the supply was, the demand was greater. His work was collected by a relatively few individuals, and so few originals ever became available to the public. Still, Russell never really received the full fruits of his labors, financially. Pictures that he gave away or sold for a paltry few dollars in the 1880s and 1890s were worth many times that 20 years later.

Russell used no models for his paintings. His knowledge of Indians, cowboys, horses, and buffalo was the result of close personal observation. He never missed a chance to see Western events involving action, and, as he watched the passing of the buffalo and the Indian from the plain, he etched indelibly upon his mind the pictures he would later put onto canvas and cast in bronze.

Even as a boy, Russell habitually carried clay or beeswax in his pocket, using it to mold small animals or other objects. Yet, although his paintings brought him worldwide fame, his sculptures were seldom seen by the public. The original clay models were extremely fragile and could be moved from place to place only at great risk. Casting them into bronze was expensive, placing a definite limitation on their reproduction.

There are some collectors who believe he was more talented as a sculptor than a painter, perhaps because sculpting is a more difficult form of artistic expression. Because the model can be viewed from every angle, it must be perfect in proportion, position, and detail.

In his sculpting, Russell began where most artists stopped: Where another sculptor might model a horse, for example, Russell would model a bucking bronc, twisted into an unusual and difficult position. His modeling shows a wild freedom of action that few sculptors would attempt.

Several of Russell's models have been preserved in bronze. The first, cast in 1904, was entitled *Smoking Up*. It portrayed a cowboy on a rearing horse, shooting up the town. Fewer than 20 of his sculptures involve group action. One of the largest of these is called *Counting Coup*, or *When Sioux and Blackfeet Meet*, depicting a group of warriors in a ferocious battle. His subjects were usually cowboys, Indians, and animals, but a few were distinguished friends, such as Will Rogers and Douglas Fairbanks.

At the time of his death, Russell was working on a model of a stage driver seated upon a great Concord drawn by six fast horses. For this piece he had selected the title *It Ain't No Lady's Job*, in honor of those sturdy men.

Russell loved the Old West, and he loved everyone who shared his affection. It was the cement that bound him to men in all walks of life—men like Will Rogers, Teddy Roosevelt, Emerson Hough, Harry Carey, Frank Linderman, and Douglas Fairbanks.

One of Russell's respected friends was Judge James Bollinger of Davenport, Iowa, who came West in the fall of 1918 for the first of several big-game hunts. He met Russell through his former classmate from Iowa State University, John Lewis, who operated the Lake McDonald Lodge in Glacier National Park. The three men shared a deep affection for the outdoors, and whenever they could they got together for a fall hunt in the Montana Rockies.

The Russells had no children of their own, but they adopted a baby boy in 1916. Russell loved fatherhood, but beginning in 1920 his health began to deteriorate. In 1924, he suffered a severe attack of sciatic rheumatism. His physicians suggested that he spend his winters in a warmer climate, and so the Russells began migrating to Los Angeles for the winter. They were building a home in Pasadena at the time of his death.

In the summer of 1926, Russell went to the Mayo Clinic in Rochester, Minnesota, where he underwent a goiter operation and learned that he did not have long to live. He died October 24, 1926, in Great Falls and was buried there.

Many honors have been accorded Russell. The University of Montana conferred upon him an honorary law degree in 1925. On August 4, 1928, in keeping with Russell's will, Mrs. Russell deeded her Great Falls property to the city for a memorial to the great artist. This included the family home and log studio, all his personal effects and working equipment, and a rare collection of cowboy and Indian curios. The house has been designated a national historic site. In 1931, a life-sized bust of Russell was added to the memorial.

Under a congressional act of 1864, each state is entitled to have statues of two of its citizens in the Statuary Hall of Fame in Washington, D.C. Montana chose Charlie Russell for that honor, and a seven-foot statue of Russell by John B. Weaver was unveiled in the hall on March 19, 1959—the 95th anniversary of Russell's birth.

Russell is estimated to have produced about 2,600 works of art in his lifetime, including paintings, drawings, and sculptures. Undoubtedly, many are in the hands of individuals. However, the bulk of his work is held by a few institutions, including the Amon Carter Museum of Western Art in Fort Worth, Texas; the Thomas Gilcrease collection in Tulsa, Oklahoma; the C. M. Russell Museum and Art Gallery in Great

Falls, Montana; and the Montana Historical Society in Helena, Montana.

The Great Falls museum is a nonprofit establishment built in 1953 to house the Josephine Trigg[10] collection of art and Russell memorabilia. The museum, together with the home and log-cabin studio, form a major Great Falls tourist attraction and community art center.

The Amon Carter Museum, named for a Texas oil man, contains Carter's collection of Russell's work, which is valued at $2 million.

The Montana Historical Society's collection of Russell art dates from 1909, when the artist himself donated the classic watercolor *York*. In 1952, a magnificent group of works was sold by the family of Malcolm S. Mackay, a New York stockbroker, Montana rancher, and friend of Russell. Since then, the collection has nearly doubled. One of the pieces acquired in the past 30 years is the masterpiece entitled *When the Land Belonged to God*, a 42½-by-72-inch canvas that depicts a herd of buffalo fording the Missouri River. In 1914, the Montana Club in Helena paid $3,000 for the picture, and in 1977 it was sold to the state for $450,000.

Russell's greatest masterpiece is generally considered to be his 11-by-24-foot mural of *Lewis and Clark Meeting the Flathead Indians at Ross Hole*. It was commissioned by the state of Montana in 1911 for $5,000. Today, it is valued at more than a million dollars. It hangs behind the rostrum in the House Chamber of the Capitol. Thus, two of Russell's greatest paintings have been kept in Montana and may be viewed by the public in Helena.

Though Russell's art forms a lasting tribute to the man, it is not the only thing for which he is remembered. Will Rogers once said of the artist, "Charlie Russell would have been a great man if he couldn't have painted a fence post."

10

Walter McClintock

Chief Mad Wolf's Adopted Son

A Blackfeet chief adopted the noted ethnologist Walter McClintock because he wanted a white son who could promote tribal interests among policymakers in the East. Because of his intimacy with the Blackfeet, McClintock was able to help preserve a culture that otherwise might have been lost. *Courtesy of Montana Historical Society*

Walter McClintock was intensely interested in the culture and welfare of the Blackfeet Indians. He lived among them from 1896 to 1900 and intermittently for several years thereafter, and much of this time was spent in or near what is now Glacier National Park. He remained an admirer of and regular visitor to the park throughout his long and unusual career.

McClintock was born April 25, 1870, in Pittsburgh, Pennsylvania, the second son of Olive and Clara McClintock. He received his early education at the Shadyside Academy, which his father helped to found, and he graduated from Yale University in 1891. His alma mater bestowed an honorary master's degree upon him in 1911, in recognition of his valuable contributions to the science of ethnology.

In the spring of 1896, he went to northwestern Montana as part of a government expedition charged by President Grover Cleveland with recommending a national policy on the creation of forest preserves. The expedition was composed of Gifford Pinchot, chief of the U.S. Forest Service and later governor of Pennsylvania, and Henry S. Graves, later chief forester of the United States and dean of the Yale School of Forestry. McClintock went along as a photographer and to help with the forest surveys. The party engaged two guides. One was Billy Jackson, a grandson of Hugh Monroe and former scout for the U.S. Army under General Custer. He was a quarter Blackfeet. The other was Jack Monroe, a white man unrelated to Hugh Monroe who had married into the Blackfeet tribe.

The members of the expedition examined the forests in northwestern Montana, both on the eastern and western slopes of the Rocky Mountains. They surveyed the country where the Flathead Forest Reserve was later established and also the region that became Glacier National Park. At the time, the country was wild and empty, visited only by Indians, trappers, a few hunters of big game, and an occasional prospector.

When the expedition concluded its survey, Graves set out for Kalispell, while Pinchot and Jack Monroe started south for Fort Missoula. McClintock and Jackson crossed the mountains at Cut Bank Pass and headed for the camp of the Pikuni branch of the Blackfeet, which was gathered on the plains for the annual Sun Dance ceremony. The visit was to change McClintock's life.

Jackson brought McClintock, then about 26 years old, to the lodge of the head chief, White Calf, and his wife, Catches-Two-Horses, the givers of the Sun Dance ceremony. They talked with the venerable chief, Running Crane, and saw his wife who was fasting because of a vow to the sun. They went to the tipis of the war chiefs, Little Plume and Little Dog, and smoked a friendly pipe, and they went to visit the judges, Shoots-the-Air, Curly Bear, and Wolf Plume, as well as the medicine men, White Grass and Bull Child. McClintock also met Chief Mad Wolf, a renowned orator and owner of the ancient beaver bundle, one of the essential parts of an important Blackfeet religious ceremony.

After attending the Sun Dance, McClintock and Jackson went to the latter's ranch in the valley of the Cut Bank River, not far from the homes of chiefs White Calf and Mad Wolf and medicine men White Grass and Ear Rings.

Jackson had a cabin built of pine logs from the mountains, with a sod-covered roof and clay-chinked walls. His wife was an Indian woman named White Antelope, and the couple had four children. The family slept in one room, McClintock in the other. In good weather, he slept outside the cabin under the stars, on the grassy bank of the river.

It was haying time, and Jackson, McClintock, and a young relative of Jackson's named Yellow Bird mowed, raked, and stacked about 80 tons of hay at the ranch. Then, Yellow Bird and McClintock rode the range after stray horses and cattle, and later they tried their hand at breaking in a new team of horses for the wagon. When Jackson needed timber from the mountains, McClintock and Yellow Bird, with two teams and wagons, cut and loaded many large trees and brought them down the steep roads to the ranch.

When all these chores were finished, McClintock and Yellow Bird set off for Alberta, Canada, where they visited Yellow

Bird's relatives at a camp of the Kainah Indians. McClintock was invited to take an Indian wife and join the tribe, but after a brief visit, he and his friend returned to the Jackson ranch. McClintock recalled going one evening with White Antelope to visit her mother, the widow of Four Bears, who had been an influential medicine man in the tribe. Her name was Two-Bear-Woman and because she was Jackson's mother-in-law, tribal custom forbade any dealings or even conversation between the two.

McClintock paid frequent visits to the nearby summer camp of the Blackfeet. He wanted to see them in their natural setting and talk with them about their day-to-day life. He began to enjoy their confidence when they saw that he was not critical of them.

Near the end of summer, McClintock met Mad Wolf on the prairie. The chief was alone and gave a sign that he wanted to talk to McClintock. After they had shaken hands, Mad Wolf looked earnestly into the young man's face and told him that he had been much impressed by him and wanted to adopt him as a son. McClintock, although taken by surprise, responded that he would like to be his son, and they arranged to meet at Mad Wolf's lodge the following morning for the adoption ceremony.

The next day, McClintock rode his favorite horse, Kootenai, into the Blackfeet summer camp. He dismounted and entered the lodge to find a number of Indians already seated, including Blessed Weasel, Heavy Breast, Double Runner, Middle Calf, Bear Child, and Many-White-Horses. The men were all at Mad Wolf's left, while the women and children were seated at his right. Between Mad Wolf and his wife, Gives-to-the-Sun, who sat on his immediate right, lay the sacred beaver bundle, opened only in a religious ceremony or on other important occasions.

After beginning the adoption ceremony with a prayer, Mad Wolf opened the beaver bundle and motioned to McClintock to kneel while he prayed on his behalf. Then, all joined in a chant and in the song of the war eagle, after which Mad Wolf brought the ceremony to a close with a final prayer. After a feast of soup made of serviceberries and beef tongue, the participants rose and filed out of the lodge.

Less than a month later, when the moon was full, Mad Wolf held a second ceremony for the purpose of giving McClintock an Indian name and making him a member of the Blackfeet tribe. The guests, who began to arrive when the sun was high over the eastern horizon, included the principal men of the tribe: White Calf, Elk Chief, Bear Child, Ear Rings, and Double Runner. The tipi was filled to the door with 11 men, 17 women, and 10 children.

Incense was burned, the beaver bundle was opened, and a series of chants followed, after which Mad Wolf and White Grass danced a special dance. The opening of the sacred bundle revealed the skins and relics of many birds and animals, from among which a beaver skin was taken. The women danced in front of the bundle, holding the beaver skin reverently and imitating the movements of beavers. After prayers and more chanting, two winter weasel skins were held up, and the Weasel Song was sung. Chief White Calf rose, took one of the snow-white skins, stopped in front of McClintock, and said earnestly:

This is the white weasel, one of the sacred animals in our beaver bundle. We name you "A-pe-ech-e-ken" [White-Weasel-Moccasin], because your color is light [he was blond] and your eyes are blue. We pray this name may bring you long life and good luck.

After dozens more songs and dances, the ceremony finally ended and the guests prepared to go home, first partaking of a feast of serviceberry stew. Peace and quiet settled over the camp, and McClintock was now a full member of the tribe.

Thus, within a few brief months of his arrival in Montana, the young Easterner had achieved the rare distinction of becoming the adopted son of a Blackfeet chief, as well as a warmly welcomed member of one of the proudest tribes on the American continent. Less than a year before, he had never heard of the Blackfeet, nor had he felt any urge to live in the Northwest or to devote himself to studying ethnology on the frontier.

Mad Wolf had a reason for adopting White-Weasel-Moccasin as his son. He saw the ever-encroaching tide of white settlers and predicted the eventual disintegration of his tribe. Many white men were shrewd and unprincipled, and he wanted a son among the white man upon whom he could depend, one who could go to the Great Father in Washington and intercede on behalf of the Blackfeet.

So McClintock was introduced to the inner circle of tribal life. He made friends with the chiefs and medicine men. He accompanied the Blackfeet on their travels and hunting expeditions and became intimately associated with their family life. Through their openness, he was able to record much about their civilization. With graphophone, notebook, and still and moving-picture camera, he gathered an extensive and valuable record of the life, legends, and sun worship of this tribe of northwestern Montana and southern Alberta.

The Blackfeet had no written language and no native historian other than storyteller James Willard Schultz. But for McClintock's work, an entire culture might have been lost.

McClintock compiled his knowledge into a series of popular lectures, accompanied by pictures, Indian songs, and beautiful, colored photographic lantern slides. His lectures were heard with interest and enthusiasm in Germany, England, Scotland, Ireland, Denmark, and the United States.

In Germany, he gave a series of lectures to the Berlin Society for Anthropology, Ethnology, and History in the Imperial Museum Voelkerkunde. He lectured at the U.S. Embassy in Berlin, as well as before the imperial ministers of the German Emperor, ladies in waiting of the Empress, ambassadors of foreign countries, and military and naval attaches. He was invited to dine with the German Crown Prince and Princess at their Berlin Palace, and he gave a lecture before members of the imperial family and their friends at the Marble Palace in Potsdam, Germany.

McClintock also gave a series of lectures at the Royal Institute in London, at the Royal Society of Dublin, and at the Universities of Oxford and Cambridge. In the spring of 1907, he was invited to give a lecture before President and Mrs. Theodore Roosevelt in the historic East Room of the White House. The distinguished guests included members of the cabinet, the Supreme Court, the diplomatic corps, and other notables.

McClintock wrote several books about the Blackfeet. The first, and perhaps the most notable, was *The Old North Trail*. It contained a vivid portrait of Indian social life and an accurate record of their legends, ceremonies, and sun worship. It was published by McMillan and Company, of London, England, and was translated into German under the title *Das Schwannenlied des Roten Kriegers* (The Swan Song of the Red Warriors). The type had been set and the proof sheets had been read when World War I intervened and caused indefinite postponement of the German version.

A reviewer of *The Old North Trail* wrote in the *London Times*:

Mr. McClintock gives us a thousand charming pictures—a few reproductions in color of excellent

*drawings, many more the work of his camera, but most
and best of all, prose descriptions irradiated with the*
joie de vivre *of the nomadic life of the foothills . . . His
book is a mirror, in which the soul of the red man, mis-
understood for so many generations of his conquerors,
is faithfully reflected, and yet is luminous with light
from within.*

In *Nation*, a London publication, R. B. Cunningham-Graham
wrote:

*Many have written of what they saw and told us of their
sports, the wars, the loves and pastimes of these people
of the Stone Age, but, since the days of Hunter, only
the writer of the present volume has told us of their
souls and their interior life. This book and Hunter's are
perhaps the best books that have been written on the
American Indians.*

A writer in the *Standard of London* had the following
to say:

*The extraordinary interest and value that are attached
to this book have their foundation in the fact that no
such book can ever be written again. The Blackfeet
Indians of Alberta and Northwestern Montana are a
dying race . . . The book must take its place among the
standard works of ethnology.*

McClintock wrote several other books dealing with the
Blackfeet. One was *Old Indian Trails*, an account of his life
with the Pikuni Blackfeet, published by Constable and Company of London in 1923. Others in English were *The Tragedy of*

*the Blackfeet, Blackfoot Tipi, The Beaver Bundle, Dances of the
Blackfeet, The Warrior Societies,* and *Painted Tipis and Picture
Writing.* Published in German were *Lebens Brauche, Legenden
der Schwarzfuss Indianer,* and *Medizinal und Nutzflanzen der
Schwartzfuss-Indianer.*

In the winter of 1913–14, McClintock made his seventh
trip to Europe to lecture before popular audiences in Berlin
and Copenhagen. Because of the favorable attention given his
lectures by the Berlin press, scientific societies and theaters
arranged for his appearance throughout Germany, Austria, and
Hungary. He had to abandon the tour, however, because of the
outbreak of World War I.

The Blackfeet were a musical people, and McClintock preserved a number of their songs for posterity. Several of their
sacred hymns, war songs, and love and night songs are contained in *The Old North Trail.*

In 1905, McClintock persuaded the American composer,
Arthur Nevin, to visit the camps of the Blackfeet with him, and
he suggested the composition of an opera founded upon the
ancient Blackfeet legend of Poia (Scarface). Nevin completed
the opera called *Poia,* in the spring of 1906, using a libretto
by Randolph Hartley, of New York City. The premiere performance took place April 23, 1910, at the Berlin Royal Opera
House. Three other performances followed, one of which was
attended by the Crown Prince and Princess and other members of the royal family. The opera received special praise from
scholars as well as from high officials of the German court.

In recognition of the value of McClintock's work, the U.S.
Geological Survey on February 7, 1912, conferred his name
upon a peak in Glacier National Park. Mount McClintock, the
first peak along the Continental Divide north of Cut Bank Pass,
rises to a height of 8,285 feet. In 1925, when James Willard
Schultz and his Indian friends recommended the restoration of

Blackfeet names to the natural features of the park, they suggested that Mount McClintock be called Bull Trail Mountain. Bull Trail was "a noted warrior in the long-ago time when the tribes of the Blackfeet Confederacy were driving the Crows south to the Yellowstone."[11]

Schultz apparently was unaware of McClintock's great friendship with the Blackfeet. In his story of Mad Wolf, he makes no reference to the chief's adoption of the white man.[12] Nonetheless, Mount McClintock is still on the official maps of the park.

In the 1930s and early 1940s, McClintock came to Glacier National Park every summer. He spent his time walking the trails and talking with old Indian friends. In the summer of 1936, he identified the location of the "old north trail" in the vicinity of East Glacier, saying it ran across what is now the seventh fairway of Glacier's nine-hole golf course.

In his later years, McClintock served as a lecturer at Yale University and as a fellow in ethnology at the Southwest Museum, Los Angeles. The museum published in pamphlet form a series of his Indian studies. His photographs of Blackfeet Indian life, taken during his years with the tribe and enlarged and colored under his personal direction, became a permanent exhibit at both Yale and the Southwest Museum. The photographs are perhaps the most comprehensive record of any Indian people.

McClintock regarded Pittsburgh as his permanent home, although he remained unmarried and spent much time away from the city. He died March 24, 1949, and was buried in the Allegheny Cemetery there.

11
Louis Warren Hill
Godfather to Glacier

As president of the Great Northern Railway, Louis Warren Hill did more than any other man to put newly created Glacier National Park on the map. He directed the construction of hotels and chalets, roads, and trails, and he launched a phenomenal publicity campaign to lure tourists to the park, coining the slogan "See America First." *Courtesy of Minnesota Historical Society*

The man who did more than any other to put Glacier National Park on the map, to enhance its scenic and recreational appeal, and to make its name a byword with the traveling public was Louis Warren Hill. In depth of devotion to the region and multiplicity of contributions to its development, he had no peer. Yet, by all but park history buffs, the record of his amazing accomplishments has been forgotten, and no adequate account of them currently exists. In all of Glacier's more than 1,500 square miles, there is no peak, pass, lake, valley, or road named for this remarkable park pioneer.

Other leading parks have had their outstanding sponsors and benefactors: Nathaniel P. Langford, often called the father of Yellowstone, John Muir for Yosemite, George W. Stewart for Sequoia, Will G. Steel for Crater Lake, and Enos Mills for Rocky Mountain. All were endowed with an abundance of dedication, determination, and imagination. So was Louis Hill. But Hill's contributions to Glacier were unquestionably greater because he had the financial means to convert his dreams into reality. With a giant transportation system—the Great Northern Railway—at his disposal, he could take steps to initiate many park projects that might have been delayed for years if left to the government.

One source estimated that, in the first five years of the Park's existence, Hill spent almost $10 there for every one spent by the government.

Hill was a son of the famed "Empire Builder," James J. Hill, and he succeeded his father in the presidency of the Great Northern Railway in 1907, just as the movement to create a national park in northwestern Montana was getting under way. In a matter of months, he had put all the forces of his company into the fight to persuade Congress to act. His motivation was not entirely altruistic, for passenger traffic was then a major contributor to railroad revenues throughout the country, and the development of an outstanding scenic attraction along the very border of a transcontinental railroad promised a substantial boost in profits.

Hill stated frankly, in a speech to the first national-park conference held in 1911: "The railroads are greatly interested in the passenger traffic to the parks. Every passenger that goes to the parks, wherever he may be, represents practically a net earning." He realized, however, that this was true only if travel in the park was both possible and comfortable.

So, once the bill to create Glacier National Park was approved by the president May 11, 1910, Hill organized a subsidiary, the Glacier Park Hotel Company, to begin building facilities for tourists. Under his personal direction, bold and imaginative plans were drawn for a chain of "forest" lodges and chalets at strategic points throughout the park. As a result, the great Glacier Park Hotel was completed in time for the 1913 summer season and the Many Glacier Hotel in 1915. Hill was also involved in the construction of the Prince of Wales Hotel, which opened in 1927 in neighboring Waterton Lakes National Park in Canada.

Another critical need of the fledgling park was decent roads. When the government failed to construct them, Hill again stepped into the breach. Using Great Northern funds, with the promise of eventual reimbursement by the Department of the Interior, Hill built the original road along the eastern border of the park, leading from what is now East Glacier to Swiftcurrent Lake (then called Lake McDermott). He also built stub roads into the Two Medicine and Cut Bank Valleys.

Hill was likewise a prime mover in the development of some of the park's early scenic trail facilities. At his bidding and with Great Northern money, the trail from the Glacier Park Hotel over Mount Henry into the Two Medicine Valley was constructed in 1913. In 1902, before creation of the park, his father had sponsored construction of a trail from Lake McDonald to Sperry Glacier and Gunsight Pass, making Great Northern funds and materials available to Lyman B. Sperry for that purpose. But it was Louis, many years later, who recognized the possibilities of a route over Red Gap Pass to the Belly River country, and he persuaded the National Park Service to construct the trail in the early 1920s.

Among the greatest of Hill's accomplishments on behalf of the park was the phenomenal publicity he gave it. He coined the slogan "See America First" and used it to promote passenger travel to Glacier. He also conceived the idea of using the Rocky Mountain goat, symbol of the park, as a part of the famous Great Northern trademark, seen for decades on the company's rolling stock, timetables, and advertising brochures. As Freeman H. Hubbard, editor of *Railroad* magazine, observed: "Few symbols in America are better known than the Great Northern goat. It is generally regarded as a million dollar idea."

Hill initiated an advertising campaign featuring the park's attractions that had few equals in its time. Of this extraordinary publicity drive, a contemporary wrote: "As a drummer up of trade for Uncle Sam's newest sideshow, he was about to make all previous performers on the tautened cowhide sound like the guitar thrummers at a sociable for the deaf."

The motion-picture industry was used effectively to film the park's sensational scenery for weekly newsreels. The Blackfeet Indians were brought into the act to provide colorful foregrounds for these pictures. Blackfeet chiefs were also taken east to Chicago and New York, where they proved to be sensational newsmakers. In New York, they pitched tipis on the roof of the McAlpin Hotel, and in Chicago, they stopped traffic in the streets. They went to the Rose Carnival in Portland, to the Mardi Gras in New Orleans, and to the convention of the Mystic Shrine in Atlanta. They were photographed visiting automobile factories, prancing into the Library of Congress, and discussing policies with the president on the steps of the White House. They were even photographed shaking hands with the popular Metropolitan Opera diva, Mary Garden, on her arrival at the Union Depot in Chicago.

Valuable publicity was gained by bringing well-known organizations to the park. Invitations were extended to many geographical and mountaineering societies. The members of the Chicago Geographical Society produced an illustrated book after their visit. Special safaris were arranged for the Mazama Club of Oregon, the Mountaineers of Washington, and the Sierra Club of California.

Travelogue lecturers visited the park in order to get the material needed to present their illustrated versions of its attractions. As a result, YMCAs, clubs, and commercial organizations had a chance to hear about the park and see pictures of its incomparable scenery. Photographers distributed shots of its glaciers and lakes throughout the country—with the help of a special Great Northern press car, equipped with a photographic darkroom.

One of Hill's most spectacular ideas for publicizing the park was to have it serve as the end point for a national automobile-endurance contest called the Glidden Tour. At Hill's urging, the 1913 competition was staged over a rugged route paralleling the Great Northern right of way between Minneapolis and Glacier Park. Hill provided a special "hotel" train for participants and their fans. Besides six sleepers, two diners, and an observation car, it included a garage car with equipment for repairing automobiles and a press car fitted out with a linotype, a photoengraving plant, and mailing facilities.

The first car off the starting line was a Packard driven by Hill. He covered part of the first day's run and then quietly returned to St. Paul. On the eighth day of the race, as the drivers pulled into Poplar, Montana, they were met by a band of mounted and costumed Blackfeet braves led by host Louis Hill. He had bypassed the cavalcade by train and was joining them for the final days of the trek.

The contest was a success from every standpoint. Numerous trophies were awarded, and the coveted Glidden Cup went to a team of three Model 22 Metz roadsters that had finished with perfect scores. Last and most colorful of all the Glidden tours, it had served to draw the nation's attention to the northern route across the Great Plains and to the little-known beauty of Glacier.

The greatest publicity stunt concocted by Hill was staged in June 1913 to mark the 75th birthday of his famous father, James J. Hill. Plans were made to invite all the latter's old friends to the party, including every Great Northern engineer, conductor, brakeman, and station agent who had served the company for 25 years or more. The problem was to find a dining hall capable of comfortably seating 600 for a banquet. As the story was told by Rufus Steel in the March 1915 issue of *Sunset* magazine:

> *It was left to Louis. With each engraved invitation that went out, he enclosed a suggestion that the guest bring along an extra shirt. The party was put on a special train. The collation that celebrated James J. Hill's seventy-fifth anniversary was served in the "forest" lobby of the Glacier Park Hotel. After the walnuts and the oratory, each guest took his choice of auto, saddlehorse or climbing staff, and went for a little exercise in the interests of digestion. Whenever two or more old railroaders are gathered in the state of Minnesota, you will hear them talking about that birthday party yet.*

Louis Hill was born May 19, 1872, in St. Paul. He was the second of three sons, but the only one to achieve outstanding success in the family railroad business. He married Maud Van Courtland Taylor, and their four children were Louis Jr., Maud, James Jerome, and Courtland.

Hill was a man of many talents and interests. Educated at Exeter and Yale, he entered the railroad business in 1893,

starting at the bottom of the ladder. After five years of diversi-
fied training in 18 different jobs—including everything from
section hand and shop mechanic to general office clerk—Hill
became an assistant to his father, the president of the company.
Only nine years later, at age 35, he took over the presidency
itself, and in 1912, at the age of 40, he became chairman of the
board.

Hill and his father always had a close relationship, and
they shared a number of traits. Both had the same stocky build
and red beard, the same enthusiasm, the same loquaciousness,
the same ability to befriend the common man, and the same
talent for telling anecdotes.

Louis Hill enjoyed many things outside his business. Of
these, his family was foremost, but he enjoyed hunting, fishing,
and painting as well. He had a great love for the West and a concern for its people. During frequent business trips, he explored
the region on horseback, by wagon, and by automobile, studying the land and talking and listening to the people. Few men
knew the Indians of northwestern Montana as Hill knew them.
They called him Gray Horse, and they loved him.

Hill's interest in Glacier was not confined to its business
potential, and he became accustomed to spending part of each
summer there. He and his family usually arrived at Many Glacier in August, and often he and his sons would take pack trips
into the park's backcountry.

Many anecdotes about Louis Hill and Glacier Park exist.
Some concern his relationship to the National Park Service
and its supervision of Glacier. In the park's early years, Hill
thought the government had not expressed sufficient appreciation of the many things he had done to develop the area.
So when Mark Daniels was made general superintendent and
landscape engineer for all of the national parks, Hill invited
him on an impressive tour that left St. Paul by private railroad

car, accompanied by another car carrying an automobile and some fine saddle horses.

Starting north by car from the Glacier Park Hotel along the Lewis Range, Hill pointed to rocky Mount Henry and said to Daniels, "That's the baldest mountain top I've ever seen. Why do you suppose nothing grows up there?" Shrugging his shoulders, Daniels consulted a notebook and saw that the government had appropriated $30,000 for Glacier. "Tell you what I'll do," he said. "I'll use $5,000 of this to have trees planted up there. Maybe we can find out what's the matter."

Instead of being pleased, Hill flew into a rage and abruptly called off the trip. When he returned to St. Paul, he lodged a bitter complaint with Daniels' boss, Franklin K. Lane, the secretary of the interior. Anyone willing to use a sixth of Glacier's wretchedly inadequate appropriation to plant trees on bald Mount Henry, he said, would probably wreck the national park system. Lane took no action, since he knew Daniels had accomplished some valuable, even brilliant, things for the parks.

There were other instances in which Hill did not see eye to eye with park authorities. Following construction of the Many Glacier Hotel, the sawmill used to process most of the lumber was left standing along the shore of Swiftcurrent Lake, half a mile south of the hotel. National Park Service Director Stephen Mather let Hill know that he thought the mill had served its purpose and should be removed, along with the masses of sawdust surrounding it. When nothing had been done by 1925, Mather reminded Howard Noble, the Great Northern's park manager, that action should be taken. Noble said he needed a little more lumber, and Mather reluctantly agreed to let the mill stand a little longer.

During a trip to the park in August 1925, Mather saw that Noble still hadn't removed the mill. So he arranged for trail crews to be transported from St. Mary to Many Glacier to do the job. He invited the hotel guests to step outside for a demonstration, and he personally lighted the fuse of the first of 13 charges of dynamite. With each detonation, his mood seemed to lighten, and when people finally asked about the explosions, he said he was celebrating his daughter's 19th birthday.

When Hill learned what had happened to his property, he was reportedly furious and ready to take legal action against Mather. But mutual friends intervened, and the Great Northern finished the job of removing the mill debris. While Hill and Mather continued to respect one another, subsequent relations were said to have been something less than cordial.

Hill was exceedingly good-hearted. In the summer of 1918, a family pack trip into the Belly River region had to be cancelled at the last minute because one of his sons became ill. This made it necessary for a rancher's wife, who had come from south of the park to cook on the trip, to return home from Many Glacier Hotel, where the trip was to have begun. She learned that Hill had ordered his groom to take the saddle horses back to East Glacier, and she asked permission to ride back on one of them. Hill asked her which horse she wanted to ride and she expressed a preference for a blue mare, finest of the lot.

"If you like the blue mare," Hill said, "I'll make you a present of her." The woman was visibly overcome for a moment and protested, with tears in her eyes, that he was much too generous. He overruled her with a princely wave of the hand, explaining, "When anyone does something for Louie, she gets something of Louie's."

And so the delighted woman rode home on her own blue mare.

12

Winold Reiss

Painter of the Blackfeet

By W. Tjark Reiss with George Schriever[13]

Fritz Winold Reiss emigrated from Germany early in the 20th century and found his calling in the wilds of northwest Montana, painting portraits of the Indians. His prodigious
efforts—he once completed 34 pieces in 30 days—earned him the Indian name Beaver
Child. They also earned him a secure future in the world of art. *Courtesy of Montana
Historical Society*

Born in Germany in the latter part of the 1880s, Winold
Reiss achieved greatness as a painter in the United States,
and particularly as a painter of the Blackfeet and other Plains
Indians in and about Glacier National Park.

The road from the Black Forest, my father's birthplace, to Glacier Park, where he achieved a high point in his artistic career, was a long one. But my father's feet were already on this path in his boyhood. He knew early that he would be a painter, and his reading of the *Leatherstocking Tales* of James Fenimore Cooper and the Indian romances of Karl May convinced him that he should paint Indians. Most important for his development and fascination with the American Indians was his reading of Prince Maximilian von Wied's account of his journey to the interior of North America from 1832 to 1834 and the opportunity to study the accompanying engravings by Karl Bodmer.

Dad's first artistic schooling was with his father, and more than any other training he received, this accounted for his mastery of drawing and the speed with which he worked. When he had absorbed as much as he could from his father's teaching, he enrolled in the Royal Academy of Fine Arts and in the School of Applied Arts in Munich, which rivaled Paris as the leading art center, especially for study. He had two of the best teachers of the day, Franz von Stuck and Wilhelm von Diez. Stuck was a propagandist for modem art and exponent of the *Jugendstil*, the German equivalent of Art Nouveau. Dad was completely aware of what was going on in the art world and tried out new theories and techniques, retaining for his use those that he thought served his own art best. He felt that it was the results that counted, not the theories. His colors and composition were certainly affected by the experiments, but not to a drastic degree. In his portraits and other paintings, realism was still his aim. However, in his later designs for fabrics and rugs, he gave full play to his extraordinary abilities in abstraction. To this day, these remain as fresh and lively as if they had been newly created.

In Munich, young Winold met a fascinating and accomplished young Swiss-English woman named Henrietta Luethy, also a student in the School of Applied Arts. Both were swept off their feet, and they were married. (Henrietta was later to become a superb fabric designer and originated the idea of book jackets or "dust jackets." She taught design at the Fashion Institute of Technology in New York for many years.) Winold had performed his obligatory military service and was commissioned a reserve second lieutenant in the German army. His own plans did not include further military service, however. He wanted to paint Indians. The increasing talk of war warned him that he would have to be out of Germany soon, and in 1913 he left for the United States. His bride was expecting their child, who turned out to be me, and it was thought unwise for her to attempt the trip. She and I joined my Dad in New York three months after I was born.

When my father arrived in New York and completed the unpleasant processing through Ellis Island, he fully expected to see Indians walking about the streets of Manhattan. At least he knew that the streets were not paved with gold. He did finally meet a recognizable Indian on the "El," and got him to pose in regalia borrowed from the American Museum of Natural History. The lack of Indian subjects was only one of his many disappointments. American buyers of art were not interested in my father's modern style.

Since Mother was fluent in English, she acted as Dad's agent with art directors, editors, designers, and architects. Also, my father was fortunate in being sponsored by the Hanfstangl Gallery, one of the few galleries in New York that featured modern art. They secured several portrait commissions for him and managed for him to contribute to the magazine *Modern Art Collector*. He designed posters and fabrics, illustrated books and magazines—anything that he could put his hand to. The anti-German feeling engendered by the war was an additional obstacle which at first prevented him from making enough money to travel out West, where he now realized his subjects lived in numbers and under conditions that were more picturesque and authentic than those in New York City.

In the winter of 1919, accompanied by a student, Langdon Kihn, Dad did take off for the West, as the war was over and travel easier. Dad was still under the influence of Karl May and James Fenimore Cooper, so, when he arrived at the station platform in Browning, Montana, he picked out the most impressive-looking Indian wrapped in a buffalo robe, rushed up to him, slapped him on the back, and said "How!" The Indian, whose name was Turtle, had not had the advantages of reading about Indian forms of etiquette and was uncertain about his response. Nevertheless, Dad's good will must have carried the day, for they became good friends, and Turtle sat for him more times than any other Indian. A long-standing and close friendship developed through the years among the three of us.

Dad had trouble finding a place to stay in Browning. The only accommodations of any kind were at the Haggerty Hotel, and it was full. However, he worked out an arrangement with a cowboy who was working a night shift: Dad was able to sleep in the bed while the cowboy was out riding the range at night. Dad persuaded the people at the hotel to fit up a studio for him in one of the public rooms and started painting like fury. He was delighted to have so many good Indian subjects close at hand. He worked so hard that he earned the Indian name of "Beaver Child," producing 34 portraits in 30 days. (The entire lot was purchased by Philip Cole and is now part of the permanent collection of the Bradford Brinton Memorial Museum in Big Horn, Wyoming.)

On this trip, as on many subsequent ones, Winold used tempera and pastels rather than oils, which require time for drying and are more difficult to transport. He also preferred to use pastel and tempera to achieve the brilliant colors that he considered closer to the Indian originals.

The trip was wonderful experience and confirmed Dad's intention to paint more Indian portraits. However, back in New York, commissions were piling up, and the school he had started demanded a lot of his time. He needed help and thought of his brother, Hans Egon Reiss, who like himself, had received excellent art training in Munich. Hans hated war and loved mountain climbing and had emigrated to Sweden before World War I to avoid the former and indulge his taste for the latter. It was a hard job for Winold to persuade his brother to emigrate a second time, but eventually Hans came to New York to help run the school and to collaborate with Dad on many interior-design projects.

Uncle Hans suffered from allergies, and during summers, he was able to breathe freely only at the seaside or in the mountains. Dad suggested Glacier National Park as a retreat, and it was there that Hans went. In those days, mountain climbing was not a popular sport, but Hans got a license as a mountain guide and soon had groups of eager climbers hard at work in the park. Louis W. Hill, at that time president of the Great Northern Railway, was one of Hans' clients. The Great Northern had all manner of concessions in the park and, in order to encourage tourism there, occasionally commissioned paintings of the landscape to be reproduced in advertisements. Uncle Hans suggested to Mr. Hill that a series of portraits of local Indians done by his brother, Winold, would stimulate interest in the area. Hill agreed, and in 1927 Dad returned to Browning and Glacier National Park to paint the Blackfeet under the sponsorship of the Great Northern Railway.

The arrangement was ideal. Logistical problems were handled by the Great Northern, which had the hotel and catering concessions in the park. Our problems were to recruit Indian models and to get them to the studio and then back to their homes. Before we left New York, it was my chore to order pastels, paper, and paints—on credit. This wasn't always the easiest job. In spite of Dad's hard work, he seldom had much ready cash. The materials would sometimes run as much as $300, a considerable amount in those days. I had to convince the art suppliers that the additional credit would enable Dad to pay his entire bill in the fall after he had sold some of his summer production.

In 1927 and 1928, we made the trip from New York to Glacier National Park by rail, requiring four days. In 1929, Dad bought his first car, a Hupmobile touring model, and Uncle Hans taught him how to drive on the trip to the park. In 1930, we went by Ford Cabriolet, and later Dad bought a Cadillac, and we traveled in style if not in opulence. The Cadillac cost more to operate than Dad had anticipated, so, when we got to the park, we put the car up on blocks and said it was too good a machine to run on the dirt and gravel roads in the park. After the Cadillac experience, we shifted to Fords and stayed with them.

The trip generally required 10 days by automobile, and we often stopped by Rosebud, Rocky Boy, and Browning, Montana, to line up models. Rapid City, South Dakota, was always on the itinerary because of the excellent buffalo steaks served at the cafe there. Paved roads ended shortly after St. Paul. That meant we drove more than a thousand miles on washboard, gravel, and dirt roads, some of which were under construction or repair. Rain was another enemy. We seemed to spend as much time getting out of the mud as we did moving along the road. Old-timers like myself will recall with satisfaction the ingenuity with which we overcame ruts, high road crowns, creeks, bogs, untrustworthy bridges, and animals, both domestic and wild. Sometimes a local entrepreneur would pull us out of or through the mud for $10, which was considered gouging. A good number of farmers counted on this money and were not at all eager to see the roads improved.

Automobile tires were less than perfect, too. No motorist in his right mind would start off on a trip without plenty of "hot patches" to repair inner tubes and "boots" which fitted inside the tire and protected the inner tube in spots where the tire itself was weak. Tires were expensive, not as standard in size as they are today, and you could not count on finding the right kind of tire, especially in out-of-the-way places.

But it wasn't all heavy going, and when all went well, there was nothing to compare with the exhilaration of riding along the road and watching the world move by in a great panorama. The top of the car was usually down, and impressions therefore multiplied. It came as close to being pure joy as anything can. At least it seemed so to me then, when I was in my teens.

We always stopped in Browning, Montana. The Indians came there to draw rations allotted by the Bureau of Indian Affairs. It was the best but not the only spot to find good models. We always attended the annual Sun Dance, as this was a good opportunity to get in touch with tribes who came to the Sun Dance as guests: Crow, Cheyenne, and Chippewa sat, speaking in the sign language common to the Plains Indians. We walked around camp with the interpreter and set dates on which we could pick up the models. They were accompanied by their families, and bachelors made arrangements to stay with family groups. The Great Northern Railway provided tipis in the park for our guests and also issued rations to them. The Indians brought their own cooking and sleeping gear as well as their everyday clothes and ceremonial robes. When we picked them up at their homes on the prairie, we often had to hitch a trailer behind the touring car to accommodate the family and its belongings.

204

Negotiations with the Indians were generally simple. Dad was well known among the Blackfeet, and all of the Indians were glad to serve as models. If we were dealing with some of the other tribes, it was sometimes necessary for the interpreter to explain who Dad was and what would be involved, but in general the Indians looked upon the trip as an interesting interlude in the daily life on the reservation. We asked them to bring their ceremonial robes and medicine bundles.

After the hustle and bustle of getting the Indian models ready to leave their homes for the sittings in Glacier National Park, squeezing everyone and everything into the car and trailer, dealing with flat tires (I had to fix 40 during one summer), settling the Indians into their tipis in the park, it often happened that they would want to return home immediately. The usual reason was that the hay needed cutting. After a few days at home, they would send word that they would like to return. We soon realized that this moving about was just a part of their way of life, and we planned our schedules accordingly. I never felt foreign among the Indians. Certainly, my father's example and his acceptance by the Indians had something to do with this. They were sincere and forthright in their friendship and never tired of answering my questions. I made many Indian friends, and some I worshipped as heroes.

The painting studio was set up in a fine log lodge at the east end of Upper St. Mary Lake. When Dad and Uncle Hans started their summer school (with students coming out from New York), it was housed in the same lodge. Classes began at 9:30 each morning. Students as well as Dad and Uncle Hans often used the same model. Usually the Indians posed in their ceremonial robes. However, if they didn't have any, we would borrow fine ones from Margaret Carberry who ran the trading post at Glacier Park station. Her father had collected some magnificent Indian garments and gear; Margaret added to this collection until it was one of the greatest of its kind.

Usually the models spoke no English. If they fell asleep during, long hours of posing, one of the interpreters—Heavy Breast, Little Dog, Percy Creighton, or another—was ready to keep them awake by asking questions about their past lives and encouraging them to recount stories and legends about themselves and their people. If none of the interpreters was available, I might be called in. I would pass cigarettes to the model. Literally everyone smoked—everyone who could hold a pipe or cigar or cigarette.

Often when the Indians posed, I copied the typical designs of the moccasins or other article of clothing. These designs were unique to each tribe and represented stylized interpretations of their country, such as mountains and rivers. The designs provided an easy way to identify the models. If Dad had not completed the picture with the model posing, he would consult these drawings. Dad loved the designs on tipi linings. He had a professional appreciation of these forms and colors, and I think his delight in them can be felt in the verve and style with which he used them in his pictures.

Dad really lived up to his Indian name, Beaver Child. Once the Indian model was posed, he worked full steam ahead and seldom gave any rest periods, except to the very young or very old. The Indians were probably the best models Dad ever had, due to their serene nature. They were completely at ease and had no difficulty in staying in the same position for hours on end.

My father could do a head, such as the portrait *Mud Head*, in one morning. A portrait like *Singing in the Clouds* would require a day and perhaps a bit longer to complete the details of her costume. He worked more slowly in oils. *Chief Shot on Both Sides* probably required a week to finish. Many Indians came to the studio to see the completed portraits, and they were always welcome. They enjoyed identifying their friends and kin and were as eager to pose as Dad was to have them as models.

Uncle Hans and I received Indian names, as well as my father. Mine was Three Eagle (Neoxa Peta); Uncle Hans' was One Eagle (Neta Peta). The Indians claimed the automobile horn sounded as though it repeated his name. "Hotsy Totsy" was a favorite slang term of mine, and I was delighted that it caused a lot of laughter among the squaws. I stopped using it when the interpreter, a staid half-Scotch Blood (or Kainah) Indian, took me aside after a particular session and informed me what I had been saying all summer translated into "women's urine." For the next few days I kept a rather low profile.

The season always ended during the first week in September. My father and Hans had commitments in New York, and I had to return to school or college. The summer's production of pictures was carefully wrapped in wax paper and sent to the Great Northern Railway headquarters in St. Paul. We started the students off on their way home and said goodbye to our Indian friends. When Dad arrived in St. Paul, O. J. Magillis, advertising agent for the Great Northern Railway, would view the pictures and decide which ones they needed for the collection and which for reproduction. The first year, the GNR purchased 60 or more; the second year about 40. After the first two years, arrangements usually concerned the reproduction rights alone. Prices for the paintings ranged from $500 to $1,500, and they were used for years on the calendars which Brown and Bigelow put out for the railway, as well as in a book, *Blackfeet Indians*.

Dad's Indians appeared more and more often in public places. He incorporated some 12-feet-high Indians into his mosaic in the Cincinnati Railway Terminal, and a large number of his Indian pictures and murals were featured in restaurants of the Longchamps chain in Washington and New York. But World War II brought an end to the commissions from the Great Northern Railway, as it no longer catered to tourist traffic.

After the war, Dad wanted to move his studio out West, but his plans did not materialize. In 1950 he had his first stroke, and it seemed wiser for him to live near his physician in New York. He died there in 1953. The Blackfeet Indians scattered his ashes at the foot of the Rockies in Montana.

A Mover and a Shaker
By George Schriever

Fritz Winold Reiss (1888– or 1886–1953) was a "mover and shaker" of his time. He lived during an exciting period when old art forms were being broken up and reassembled. Born into an artistic family in the Black Forest of Germany, Reiss grew up under the dispensation of the poetic realism of Dürer, Holbein, Cranach, Grunewald, and Leibl and learned important facts from them about art forms, particularly about composition.

Winold Reiss' father was a landscape painter of note in Baden, and both Winold and his older brother, Hans Egon, studied with him. Winold was well prepared for the Royal Art Academy School and the School of Arts and Crafts in Munich, where he made excellent progress under Wilhelm von Diez and Franz von Stuck, two leading German art teachers of their day. By the time that Reiss entered the schools in Munich, the tornadoes of Cubism, Futurism, and Fauvism had begun to build up; they eventually reinforced his already strong sense of design and color.

Reiss was not affected by the Romantics, either aesthetically or emotionally, and his paintings remained free of the sentimentality of German Romantic painting. He came to maturity as Art Nouveau (*Jugendstil* in Germany) was fading away. Art Deco and Reiss came in bloom at about the same time and were well matched. Reiss adapted Art Deco to his own needs and used it consistently throughout his long and productive career. It seemed to have been made expressly to serve him in his Indian portraits. The accessories of bead and quillwork, painted Indian designs on tents and pots, baskets, parfleches, blankets, rugs, articles of clothing—on all kinds of gear and paraphernalia—might have been devised by the most modern artists of the time.

Reiss' style was already formed when he came to the United States in 1913. He did develop and refine it further, like the complete artist and craftsman that he was. Within the framework of the art of his time, using what he had learned from artists of the past, he developed a style that was so distinctive that he almost need not have signed his work. Admirers spotted it from a distance. One drawback to this robust individualism is that Reiss' pictures are hard to hang in concert with the work of other artists. I have seen hundreds of his pictures and recall less than five that were not strong enough to hold their own with any picture in the realistic tradition.

Through a combination of circumstances, not the least of which was that he adored the red man, Reiss is best known today for his portraits of the Plains Indians. But he has also painted many portraits of beautiful women, almost all of them models he chose himself. These portraits merit more general attention than they currently receive from the few enthusiasts who are now aware of them. They are honorable successors to Boldini's, which focus on the elegance of the 1890s within their frames. In the same way, Reiss' immortalize the 1920s. They are the peak of chic. The esteemed but aging Saint George Hotel in Brooklyn was given a renewed lease on life when Reiss included 13 of these portraits in his plans for redecorating that resort of the rich and famous.

Like many of his illustrious artist predecessors, Reiss designed interiors of public meeting places. Together with his brother, Hans, and a host of fine craftsmen, he planned and carried out the decoration of the Crillon Hotel in New York, the 12 Longchamps restaurants in New York, Philadelphia and Washington, the Palmer House in Chicago, and many others. Fans of his work still regret the passing of these wonderful interiors, which managed to be both stimulating and restful, a feast for the mind as well as for the eye and body.

Reiss' greatest success in interior design was within the Cincinnati Union Terminal Railway Station, a "Temple of Transportation," which was the culmination of installations of this kind. Reiss designed and executed in mosaic 14 enormous murals. They have been moved at great expense to the airport, indicating the affection that Cincinnatians have for these stupendous works of art.

Reiss' Indian portraits have been exhibited throughout the United States, Europe, and Asia Minor, a tribute to their excellence and general appeal.

13

The Clarkes and the Dawsons

Born at Fort Benton in 1859, Thomas Erskine Dawson grew up and attended schools in Scotland and England before returning to spend almost 70 years in northwestern Montana. He was known in his old age as "the last of the mountain men." *Courtesy of Joyce Clarke Turvey*

The names of two families—the Clarkes and the Dawsons—recur regularly in the annals of Montana history. Their strangely similar stories comprise a fascinating saga.

The original pioneer in each family came early to the upper Missouri River region to engage in the fur trade. Each soon found an Indian mate, and each fathered three children before 1860. Each died prematurely under unhappy circumstances.

An early settler in the Helena area, Egbert Malcolm Clarke ran a cattle ranch with his Blackfeet wife. His murder by one of her cousins precipitated the Baker Massacre of 1870, in which a band of friendly Blackfeet was wiped out by U.S. troops under the command of Major Eugene Baker. *Courtesy of Joyce Clarke Turvey*

The murder of one precipitated a massacre along the Marias River that was almost as bloody as that on the Little Bighorn.

For almost a century, members of both families have lived near the eastern border of what is now Glacier National Park. There, they have been friendly neighbors, intermarrying in one instance and even establishing their own Clarke-Dawson Cemetery.

The original Montana Clarke was Egbert Malcolm Clarke, born July 22, 1817, in Fort Wayne, Indiana. He was the only son of Lieutenant Nathaniel E. Clarke (1788–1836) and Charlotte Anne Seymour (1794–1873). Much of his early childhood was spent at the frontier outpost of Fort Snelling, near what is now Minneapolis.

Shortly before his 17th birthday, Malcolm Clarke entered West Point, where he was a schoolmate of General William T.

Sherman of Civil War fame. When his high-spirited conduct (he even challenged a fellow cadet to a duel) led to his dismissal, he traveled to Texas to join its fight for independence from Mexico. He was commissioned a lieutenant by Sam Houston and served to the end of the hostilities.

In 1841, Clarke headed for the Northwest, where he got a job with the American Fur Company with the help of his father's lifelong friend, Alexander Culbertson. Before long, he had won the admiration and respect of the Indians by killing four grizzly bears in one day. For this feat, they named him Four Bears. He eventually established a company post at Fort Benton and worked there for a number of years.

When Clarke left the fur-trading business, it was with the idea of entering the cattle business, and he bought a ranch near Helena at the mouth of the Little Prickly Pear Canyon. In the meantime, he had acquired a family. In about 1844, he took as his mate a woman about 10 years his junior named Cothco-co-na, the daughter of a Pikuni chief. They became the parents of Helen, born in 1846, Horace in 1848, Nathan in 1852, and Isabel in 1861. A second wife of mixed blood, Good Singing Sandoval, became the mother of daughter Judith, also born in 1861. By 1869, he and all his children were living at his ranch, known today as the Sieben Ranch and owned by the Baucus family.

Because of his integrity and geniality, Clarke was well-liked by both Indians and whites. However, he did have a few enemies, including a cousin of his wife named Pete Owl Child (Ne-tus-che-o). On the evening of August 17, 1869, Owl Child and some of his friends came to the Clarke home, ostensibly on a friendly visit. Clarke invited them to stay for dinner and treated them with cordiality, but Owl Child fatally shot Clarke, and another of his party shot Clarke's son, Horace. The latter was seriously wounded and left for dead, but he eventually recovered. The rest of the family escaped unharmed, although they, too, had been marked for death.

The incident happened not long after other depredations by irresponsible Blackfeet who could not be controlled by their chiefs. As a result, residents of the area complained so much to the federal government that it finally decided to punish the culprits, who were believed to have taken refuge in the camp of Mountain Chief's band of Blackfeet wintering on the Marias River.

Major Eugene E. Baker was given command of about 350 mounted men and ordered to find and wipe out Mountain Chief's band. He was expressly instructed to avoid attacking any other band of Indians, and young Joseph Kipp, who was familiar with the Blackfeet, was sent with Baker to make sure he knew which band was which. At dawn on January 23, 1870, the troops came upon a sleeping Indian camp which Kipp warned Baker was that of Chief Heavy Runner, a friendly band. Nevertheless, Baker ordered his men to attack, and the carnage began.

Fatalities were heavy. Army reports agreed that 173 were killed but disagreed on how many were women and children. The tragedy, which became known as the Baker Massacre, caused an uproar in Congress and throughout the eastern part of the country, but it met with less disapproval in Montana. It served to break the spirit of the Blackfeet, making life easier for settlers on the frontier. Major Baker was not punished for his flagrant disobedience, while Owl Child, who escaped retribution at the hands of Baker's troops, died shortly thereafter of smallpox.

As for Malcolm Clarke, while he is more likely to be remembered as the victim of the cold-blooded murder that precipitated the Baker Massacre, he should also be remembered for the interesting and talented Montanans whom he fathered.

Helen Clarke

One of the most gifted of Malcolm's offspring was his first child, Helen Pioto-po-wa-ka, who was born October 11, 1846, while her parents were living at an outpost of the American Fur Company at the mouth of the Judith River. She was baptized in the Catholic faith and remained a devout member of the church throughout her life.

Clarke sent his children East for their education, and Helen lived for a time with an aunt in Minneapolis, where she attended convent schools. She received further schooling while living with another of her father's relatives, Mary Lincoln, in Cincinnati, after which she attended a school of drama in New York City. Nellie, as Helen was known to her friends, grew to be a rather large woman with a crown of dark hair, a strong aquiline nose, and piercing black eyes. Her voice was deep and vibrant, contributing to her powers as a teacher, actress, and administrator.

Shortly after she finished drama school, she embarked upon a meteoric stage career. Friends have described an album in which she kept press notices about her appearances in New York, London, Paris, and Berlin, including an appearance with Sarah Bernhardt in a Shakespearean role. The album also contained a letter from the German kaiser, commending her portrayal of Lady Macbeth, and a letter from the queen of the Netherlands. Nevertheless, she was not happy as a thespian, for she soon returned to Montana to devote most of her remaining years to public service.

Helen spent many years teaching in the schools of Fort Benton and Helena. She was nominated in 1882 by the Republican party for the post of superintendent of schools of Lewis and Clark County. The nomination was endorsed by the Democrats, and Helen became the first woman ever elected to public office in Montana. She was re-elected in 1884. She was also a charter member of the Montana Historical Society and made a number of contributions to it.

In 1891, Helen was recruited by the Office of Indian Affairs to serve as an interpreter and mediator in allotting land to the Blackfeet under the federal Indian Allotment Act of 1887. Helen was so successful that she was sent to Oklahoma to work with the Ponca, Otoe, Pawnee, and Tonkawa Indians. She served in this capacity from 1891 to 1899, with the exception of 1895 and 1896, when she returned to the Blackfeet reservation to help her people prepare the treaty with which they sold to the United States, for $1.5 million, the part of the reservation that lay east of the Continental Divide in what is now Glacier National Park.

"Aunt Helen," as she came to be known, never married. In 1902, she moved in with her brother, Horace, who had built one of the first homes in Midvale, which is now East Glacier Park. The home, with its fine library of books, was a rendezvous for many notables, such as the Western artist, Joseph H. Sharp, and Helen Fitzgerald Sanders, who dedicated *The White Quiver* to Helen and Horace. Helen died March 5, 1923, and was buried in the Clarke-Dawson Cemetery at East Glacier Park.

Horace and Isabel Clarke

Malcolm Clarke's older son, Horace, was born in 1848, possibly at Fort Benton. Like his sister, he spent some years at school in Minneapolis, where he was sent to live with his father's sister, Charlotte Van Cleve. After returning to Montana, he became a victim of the Owl Child conspiracy to murder his father. Horace narrowly escaped death after being shot in the face by the elder son of Mountain Chief. Although the bullet entered his mouth and emerged near his ear, Horace recovered in time to serve, along with his brother, Nathan, with the troops sent out under Major Baker to avenge their father's death.

In 1875, Horace left the family ranch and homesteaded on Indian land that is now part of the Harris Ranch near Highwood, Montana. About this time, he married Margaret Full Kill, a Blackfeet woman. They had a daughter and seven sons, five of whom died in infancy, probably from scarlet fever. The survivors were Malcolm (1877–1922), Agnes (1883–1975), and John Lewis (1881–1970).

In 1888, Horace was granted 160 acres of land under the federal Indian Allotment Act of 1887. His acreage was northwest of what became the Great Northern Railway right-of-way at what is now East Glacier Park. More than 20 years later, he sold 60 acres to the railroad company to serve as the site of its Glacier Park Lodge and golf course. Horace raised hay and cattle on his property. From time to time, he also worked as an army scout, cowboy, and mountain guide. He became a tribal leader and headed a minority faction that in 1895–96 opposed the sale of Blackfeet land to the government. Horace died at East Glacier Park in 1930 and was buried in the Clarke-Dawson Cemetery.

Malcolm's second daughter, Isabel Agnes, or Cothco-co-na, was born August 25, 1861. Following the death of her father in 1869, she went with her half-sister, Judith, to live with their aunt, Charlotte Van Cleve, in Minneapolis. There they were educated at St. Joseph's Academy, from which Isabel graduated in music. The sisters returned to Montana in the early 1880s to live with their brother, Horace, so that Isabel could help care for their invalid mother. After their mother's death, Isabel became a governess for the family of Major Peter Ronan, agent for the Flathead Indians. Later, she was asked by Major Baldwin, a Blackfeet agent, to act as matron and teacher at Old Agency.

In about 1889, while working at Old Agency, Isabel met Thomas Dawson, who was also employed by the Indian Service. They were married in 1891, and in 1893 they moved to an allotment of acreage at the mouth of Marias Pass. They continued to live there for many years. The town of Midvale, now East Glacier Park, was established on what had been their property, and the couple eventually moved there from their ranch home. The Dawsons adopted two girls, Mary Lorena Young Meade (1888–1967) and Helene Patterson Edkins (1898–1986), the daughter of Isabel's half-sister, Judith. Isabel died April 3, 1935, and was buried in the Clarke-Dawson Cemetery.

One of Montana's first pianos was brought West in the 1880s by Isabel, who loved music. It remained in her homes and that of her daughter, Helene, for more than 80 years, until Helene arranged for it to be taken in 1972 to the Fort Benton museum, where it can be seen today.

John Clarke

Another of Malcolm Clarke's talented descendants was his grandson, John Lewis Clarke, who became one of the greatest woodcarvers of his time. He was born May 10, 1881, in Highwood, Montana, near Great Falls, and he died November 20, 1970, only six months short of his 90th birthday. His father was Horace Clarke and his mother was Margaret Full Kill, the Blackfeet daughter of Chief Stands Alone.

At age two, John contracted scarlet fever, a malady that deprived him of his sense of hearing and his ability to speak. He received his education at several institutions, including the Montana School for the Deaf at Boulder, the North Dakota School for the Deaf at Devil's Lake, and the St. John's School for the Deaf at Milwaukee, Wisconsin. By none of these schools, however, was he provided with any formal artistic training.

In 1913, John returned to Montana, to the vicinity of East Glacier Park, where his parents still lived. He grew familiar with the scores of wild animals which roamed the area, and he used this knowledge to create lifelike woodcarvings of them.

Although John did not embark on his career as a wood-carver until sometime after 1913, it had become his full-time occupation by 1918. In the summer of that year, he began working in a small studio near the Swiftcurrent Falls and the Many Glacier Hotel in Glacier National Park. He often signed his work with the Blackfeet name Cutapuie, which means "The Man Who Talks Not."

Someone once said of John that ". . .with an ax and a pocket knife he hews a cedar trunk out of the forest and carves the image of a bear in such reality that there is nothing missing save the growl of the ferocious-looking beast." Of course, his finer work was done with chisel and mallet.

Clarke' s wood carvings were exhibited and won honors in many galleries, including those of New York, Boston, London, Paris, and the Academy of Fine Arts in Philadelphia. His work was displayed annually at the Chicago Art Institute. In 1918, he was awarded a gold medal by the American Art Galleries of Philadelphia for a wood sculpture of a bear, and 10 years later he won a silver medal from the Spokane Art Association. He is listed in *Who's Who, American Art Annual*, volumes XVI, XX, and XXII.

During his long life, Clarke completed a prodigious number of artistic works, including four life-sized carvings of mountain goats, a standing grizzly commissioned by the Grizzly Gasoline Company, and a three-foot, four-inch bighorn sheep which is in the David Rockefeller collection along with six other pieces of his. His carvings of Montana animals were acquired by many well-known people, including former president Warren Harding, John D. Rockefeller Jr., Louis Hill Sr., and Charles Russell, a friend and admirer.

In 1940, Clarke executed large-scale panels for the Museum of the Plains Indian in Browning and for the Browning Hospital. Later, he did another for the University of Montana at

Missoula. For the Veterans' and Pioneers' Historical Building in Helena, he carved a ton of wood into a 13-by-4-foot panel in 1956.

In 1951, John was a delegate from Montana to the convention of the Washington Association for the Deaf in Seattle. In 1964, he was honored by members of the Montana Association for the Deaf with a bronze plaque commemorating his artistry in wood. The plaque was presented to the Montana Historical Society. His accomplishments have been listed in a number of books, including *Bronzes of the American West*, *Artists of the American West*, and *New Interpretations*.

John met Mary (Mamie) Peters Simon (1878–1947) in 1916 or 1917, when both were working for Tom Dawson, he as a packer, she as a cook. They were married in Columbia Falls, Montana, in 1918, and she proved to be an invaluable business partner in handling sales and exhibits of his work. In the early 1930s, they adopted a daughter, Joyce Marie, who married Irvin Turvey Jr. When Joyce inherited her father's studio near the Glacier Park Lodge, she replaced it with the attractive John L. Clarke Western Art Gallery and Memorial Museum, in which are featured the works of many Montana and out-of-state artists, as well as prizewinning photographs of Glacier National Park by Joyce herself.

Andrew Dawson

The story of the Dawson dynasty in Montana is as interesting as that of the Clarkes. Its principal characters—Andrew and his son, Thomas—grew up in Scotland 40 years apart. Each emigrated to the New World, settled in the northwest part of Montana, and attained a degree of local prominence. Although Andrew spent only 20 years on the frontier, he became known as "The King of the Missouri," and Dawson County in eastern Montana was named for him. Thomas, who was born at Fort

Benton, returned to the Northwest to spend nearly 70 years within a few miles of his birthplace. He was referred to in his old age as "the last of the mountain men."

Andrew Dawson was born April 25, 1817, near Edinburgh, Scotland. Upon completing an apprenticeship, he accepted a post as confidential clerk or secretary with a manufacturing firm in England. However, he did not stay long, as he found English ways distasteful and the business too confining.

In 1843, Andrew set sail from Liverpool for New Orleans, from whence he took a steamer to St. Louis. He got a job and soon began to hear much of the free and adventurous fur-trading life in the Northwest. As a result, after a year in St. Louis, he set forth with a companion in the direction of what is now Montana. After many hardships, he reached Fort Pierre on the Missouri River, and shortly thereafter he arrived at Fort Clark, near Bismarck, North Dakota, where he spent several years. There he met Pierre Garreau, a well-known frontiersman, and he acquired a thorough knowledge of hunting, trapping, and trading with the Indians.

After moving up the Missouri to Fort Union, Andrew met Alexander Culbertson, who in 1854 hired him to go to Fort Benton. One of his first assignments was to convert the wooden fort into a brick fortress as a safeguard against the Indians, with whom he had many perilous adventures. It was Andrew who, because of his friendship with Senator Thomas Benton, suggested renaming the post Fort Benton.

Under Andrew's management, the business of the American Fur Company at Fort Benton prospered, and he became one of the partners. In 1859, he fell and was partially crippled. The injury caused him to grow weaker every year until he almost lost the use of his legs. He decided to retire. In the summer of 1864, he handed over the fort to Matthew Carroll and George Steel, his two chief clerks.

Taking his sons, James and Thomas, with him, he traveled by water to New Orleans, where he embarked for Liverpool and then Edinburgh. He lived for a time with his brother, Ebenezer, but he later was moved by his son, James, to a private boarding house, where he died September 15, 1871, as a result of complications from his fall.

In his 20 years on the upper Missouri, Andrew acquired an assortment of Indian wives. At Fort Clark, he married Josette, the daughter of Pierre Garreau, and she became the mother of James. Years later, Mary Scott, a Brule Sioux, gave birth to his son, Andrew, probably at Fort Union. His youngest son, Thomas, was born at Fort Benton in 1859 to Pipe Woman, a Gros Ventre. James and Thomas were educated in Scotland, while Andrew was placed in the care of Robert Morgan, an old friend who lived at Fort Garry, Manitoba. Presumably, Andrew's wives were left in Montana to fend for themselves when he returned to Scotland.

Thomas Dawson

Thomas Erskine Dawson was born October 16, 1859, at Fort Benton, where he spent an unremarkable early childhood. When he was almost five, he accompanied his father and brother, James, back to Scotland.

Thomas' father wanted him to attend Oxford University in preparation for the foreign service. As a youngster, he attended a series of schools—Ruggs at Birkenhead outside Liverpool, Peebles on the River Tweed, and a third institution in Edinburgh. At age 13, Thomas attended Eton for a year, but then he was told there was no more money for his education, although his father had supposedly left enough to pay his way through the university.

So, at age 14, Thomas went to the shipyard in Glasgow, Scotland, to learn a trade. He completed an apprenticeship at age 19 and accepted employment on the Anchor Line steamer *Bolivia*, headed for New York, where he had a cousin. He left the ship there and began an odyssey that he hoped would take him to Seattle.

After working briefly in Troy, New York, and Brainerd, Minnesota, he received a letter from his brothers in Winnipeg, enclosing money he could use to join them. He worked there for a time, then headed to Fort Macleod by a roundabout route which included stops, and sometimes jobs, in Crookston, Minnesota; Fargo, North Dakota; and Billings and Fort Benton, Montana. At Fort Macleod, he joined the North West Mounted Police, who were then trying to put down the Riel Rebellion. He was stationed at Lee's Creek until July 1885. He then went south across the Canadian–U.S. border and worked as a logger with Joe Kipp until the fall of 1887, when Kipp got him a job doing maintenance work at the Blackfeet Indian Agency. He stayed there for three years, with another year of employment by Kipp sandwiched in between.

While he was working for the Indian Agency, Thomas met Isabel Clarke. They were married at St. Peter's Mission February 5, 1891, but they continued to live and work at the agency until June 1893.

In 1888, Isabel's brother, Horace, had moved onto land which would eventually border the Great Northern right-of-way on the north. Five years later, on July 1, 1893, Thomas and Isabel did the same, choosing land on the south side of the right-of-way. They built a ranch house about a mile west of the center of what is now the community of East Glacier Park, and they became ranchers.

Thomas later became a professional guide, serving, among others, Louis Hill Sr., Senator Thomas Walsh, Gifford Pinchot, and Henry L. Stimson. He pioneered all the trails in the Two Medicine Valley, into which he took many hunting parties before 1910, when the area became part of Glacier National Park. He discovered Dawson Pass. Isabel Lake was named for his wife and Helen Lake for his adopted daughter, Helene Edkins. By 1893, his wanderlust satisfied at last, Thomas was content to spend his final 60 years on his ranch on Midvale Creek, near present-day East Glacier Park.

Winold Reiss painted Thomas' picture for the Great Northern Railway, depicting him with a lugubrious expression and, much to Thomas' disgust, a coonskin cap, something he had never worn. Thomas died November 20, 1953, at age 94, and was buried in the Clarke-Dawson Cemetery.

Malcolm Clarke and Andrew Dawson had much in common. Both were born in 1817, within 90 days of each other, and both came to the upper Missouri River region in the early 1840s. Both were sponsored, although at different times, by Alexander Culbertson. Both became affiliated with the American Fur Company, and both served at Fort Benton for awhile. Both withdrew from the fur-trading business in 1864. Both were sturdy, fearless, trustworthy, capable, and genial. Both were well-liked and respected by the Indians, in large part, no doubt, because of their alliances with Indian women. Both met untimely deaths in their early 50s.

No less amazing is the number of times in Montana history that the paths of members of the two families intersected: (1) In the spring of 1861, Malcolm Clarke and Andrew Dawson spent 22 days traveling together down the Missouri from Fort Union to Council Bluffs, Iowa; (2) between 1888 and 1893, Clarke's son, Horace, and Dawson's son, Thomas, settled on adjoining tracts of Indian reservation land; (3) in 1891, Clarke's daughter, Isabel, married Dawson's son, Thomas; (4) in 1898,

Clarke's granddaughter, Helene, was adopted by Dawson's son, Thomas, and his wife; and (5) in the early 1920s, the Clarke-Dawson Cemetery was established at East Glacier Park on land owned by Clarke's son, Horace.

Endnotes

1 This is the year of her death according to James Willard Schultz in *Signposts of Adventure*, p. 51.

2 Excerpt from "The 1855 Blackfeet Treaty Council, a Memoir by Henry A. Kennerly," published in the Winter 1982 issue of *Montana, the Magazine of Western History*.

3 *William Jackson, Indian Scout*, published in 1926 by Houghton Mifflin.

4 Based largely on *Friends of My Life as an Indian*, by James Willard Schultz, pp. 76–118.

5 Varying versions of the story of the black horse appear in Schultz's books, *Friends of My Life as an Indian*, 1926, and *Blackfeet and Buffalo*, 1962. In the latter, the horse was named Puh-poom, its owner became Sleeping Thunder, and the thief was Eagle Ribs.

6 This was Grinnell's translation of the Indian name for the St. Mary lakes.

7 In *Blackfeet and Buffalo*, James Willard Schultz said Lone Wolf was given his name by Red Eagle. According to an article in *Montana, the Magazine of Western History*, Winter 1972, p. 27, Lone Wolf himself told Paul Dyck, his adopted son, that the name had been bestowed upon him by his grandfather, Yellow Wolf.

8 *Blackfeet and Buffalo*, p. 82.

9 The adventures of Lone Wolf and Angus Monroe have been described by Gordon Pouliot in *The Piegan Storyteller*, Volume VI, No.4, p. 11.

10 "Miss Josephine," as Russell called her, shared the artist's love of the outdoors and often accompanied him and Nancy on camping trips.

11 *Signposts of Adventure*, by James Willard Schultz, pp. 69–74.

12 Ibid., pp. 123–126.

13 These articles first appeared in the September/October 1981 issue of *American West* magazine and are reprinted with permission of the authors. W. Tjark Reiss, son of Winold Reiss, is an architect who lives in New York. George Schriever, a resident of New York City, is an art historian who specializes in the American West.

Index

White Antelope (Pikuni
 warrior), 98
White Antelope (wife of Billy
 Jackson), 93, 181, 182
White Bull (Cheyenne
 chief), 89
White Calf (Pikuni chief), 94,
 108, 181, 183
White Grass (Pikuni
 medicine man), 181, 183
Whoop-Up, Fort, 104
Why Gone Those Times?
 (Schultz, James W.), 133
Wilbur, Mount, 125, 148
*William Jackson, Indian
 Scout* (Schultz, James
 W.), 36
Willow Creek School, 157–58
Wind River Indian
 Reservation, 132, 136
Wolf Men (painting; Russell,
 Charles M.), 168
Wolverine, 118
Wrenn, John, 99, 113

Wrigley, Joseph, 23, 24

Yale University, 93, 138–42,
 180, 188, 194
Yanktonnais Indians, 20,
 77, 82
Yellow Bird (relative of Billy
 Jackson), 181
Yellow Fish, 123, 145
Yellow Wolf (uncle of
 Natahki), 129, 157
Yellowstone National Park,
 140, 143, 144, 154, 190
Yellowstone Park
 Improvement Co., 143
Yellowstone River, 8, 21, 51,
 65, 79, 80, 83, 95, 109,
 167, 188
Yellowstone Valley, 80, 153
York (watercolor; Russell,
 Charles M.), 178
York Factory, 5
Young, Brigham, 139

About the Glacier Association

The Glacier Association, established in 1946, has provided more than 60 years of educational and interpretive support for Glacier National Park. The mission of the non-profit association is to "Advance Stewardship of Our Natural and Cultural Heritage through Education and Interpretation," and it supports the education and interpretation programming needs of Glacier National Park as a cooperating association of the National Park Service.

When *Stars Over Montana* was originally published in 1988, Mr. and Mrs. Hanna graciously donated the manuscript, all costs of publication, and the income from book sales to the Glacier Association. The association depends upon sales and private gifts to enhance the quality of future publications and to support public programs in Glacier National Park.

For information on becoming a benefactor, helping others to understand, appreciate, and protect the values of Glacier National Park, write to the Glacier Association, P.O. Box 310, Historic Depot 12544 Highway 2 East, West Glacier, MT 59936, or visit www.glacierassociation.org.

About the Author

Warren Hanna studied the history and ecology of Glacier National Park for many years and published several books on the park in the 1970s and 1980s. He died in September 1987, and the manuscript for this book was a bequest to the Glacier Natural History Association.